# FLEXIBLE SCHEDULING

## Bold New Venture

ALREADY PUBLISHED IN THE

BOLD NEW VENTURE *Series*

*Team Teaching*
*Independent Study*
*Flexible Scheduling*

*Bold New Venture*

# FLEXIBLE
# SCHEDULING

USING

The Indi<u>F</u>lex<u>S</u> Model

*by*

*DONALD C. MANLOVE*
*and*
*DAVID W. BEGGS, III*

**INDIANA UNIVERSITY PRESS**
**Bloomington & London**

# Preface

## *Bold New Venture* Series

American education is emerging as a new frontier. Staggering challenges brought about by the contemporary demand for quality education for a bulging and diverse student population must be met. Old solutions for new problems will not suffice.

Pioneer educators are testing promising new programs and practices to effect fundamental improvement in the schools. Healthy dissatisfactions have led to the belief that if the schools are to be significantly better, they will have to be substantially different. Both the substance and the form of instruction are undergoing searching reappraisal. Exciting innovations have been instituted in schools scattered throughout the country. The *Bold New Venture* series is designed to inform educators and·the interested public about these new developments and to assist in their evaluation.

The books in this series differ from much of the professional literature in education. The contributors, for the most part, are practitioners. Admittedly they are partial to their topics. Nevertheless, pitfalls are exposed and candid treatment is given to the issues. Emphasis has been put on reporting *how* as well as *why* new practices and programs were inaugurated. The volumes in this series are intended to be a stimulus to the conversation which must take place if fresh methods of teaching are to find their way into the schools.

Topics included in the *Bold New Venture* series include team teaching, flexible scheduling, independent study, the nongraded school, instructional materials centers, data processing, small group instruction, and technological aids.

5

While journalists criticize, scholars theorize about, and philosophers analyze education, the teachers of America must act. Educators must leap from theory to practice in individualizing instruction. More responsibility must be given and accepted by youngsters for their own learning. Intellectual inquiry must become full-time, leisure-time, and life-time pursuits.

Progress in education does not always come by the process of addition with more teachers, more books, more courses, and more money. Real improvement can come from original uses of scarce human talent, precious time, and new methods.

Because it is intended primarily for teachers and administrators, the *Bold New Venture* series focuses on the practical problems of teaching. What has been operationally successful for some teachers may have application for other teachers. If new practices or programs result from these books, then the series will have fulfilled its aim, for the *Bold New Venture* books are calls and guides to action.

D.W.B.

Bloomington, Indiana                                        E.G.B.

# Contents

# Introduction

Educators do not lack grand goals or lofty motives. The history of the profession of education is blessed with both. However, a void exists in knowing how to get from theory to practice in implementing some of these noble designs. One time-honored cardinal tenet for every teacher has been to *individualize instruction.* This exhortation has been passed down from generation to generation of teachers since the early years of professional preparation courses in education. Seldom have national task forces, professional group statements, or presidential conferences failed to mention individualized teaching in one way or another.

Over the last thirty years educators have dreamed of ways to approach personalized teaching in the traditional school setting of one teacher to thirty students, give or take a half dozen. The goal has not been achieved to the satisfaction of either the profession or of the students themselves. The organization for instruction used in the schools provides for group and not individual teaching. The means—the secondary school's class schedule—is antagonistic to individualized instruction, to teaching customized to the unique requirements of each student. The time has come for the secondary schools of America to adjust the means (the organization for learning) to achieve the desired end (individualized teaching). Schools must be organized so that each individual student, with unique capabilities, interests, and background, can develop the full measure of his talent. This is not to say the schools of the past have been deficient or ineffective for their time. Evidence to the contrary carries too much to substantiate such a charge. However, the educational requirements of this new age place increased demands on the schools to offer quality customized education for every student. A widespread change in our society is taking place. Discovery in nearly every field of knowledge rises with almost every sun. Furthermore, values are far different from those of a generation ago. The world's interest has become a national and often a personal interest. The schools must help youngsters find their way in a new world which demands group interaction yet puts a heavy premium on specialized individual accomplishment.

Changes have been introduced both in how Americans work and how long they labor. Education must keep pace with these developments. Mental work has replaced physical activity in many occupations. A technological society requires precise thinking and careful consideration of narrowly intricate fields of inquiry. The early retirement age, legislated minimums in the work week, and prolonged years of schooling have reduced the amount of time an American citizen works. The emphasis in the future will be on highly specialized effort rather than on common labor. More societal adjustments are in the offing as the technological implications take hold of our society. Still, amid all this change, the schools are organized and operate in nearly the same way they have been since the first days of the Quincy Grammar School in Boston in 1848. It was a historically bold social experiment: universal educational opportunity. The moment in history has come to take another step. This one is in the direction of adding excellence to universal educational opportunity.

Somehow the goal of individualized teaching has been bypassed. The road to improvement in education up to the present has been concerned with more things—more teachers, more books, more supplies, more buildings, and more money. Correspondingly, these additions have been accompanied by the imposition of more services on the school. Quality demands on the schools, with more students to educate, are emerging as the challenge for professional educators to meet.

## IndiFlexS

On the pages that follow a model to provide quality instructional opportunity is described. The secondary school that uses a flexible schedule is taking a step, a bold first step, in getting from theory to practice in individualizing instruction. This particular application of the flexible scheduling concept is referred to as IndiFlexS, the Indiana Flexible Schedule. A label is put on it to distinguish it from other proposals which may be similar in intent but different in approach.

IndiFlexS is a model which can be used as presented, modified, or expanded, depending on the professional judgment of the practitioners concerned. At the same time, the IndiFlexS model is proposed for the study of students of public secondary school administration. Consideration is given to each of the elements in the formula a school uses for instruction—teaching talent, student learning arrangements, methods of teaching and learning, and the utilization of time and technological aids to instruction.

IndiFlexS calls for:

1. varying the rate, the depth, and the breadth of instructional opportunity for each student according to his own needs and capabilities;
2. giving teachers the opportunity to perform these functions in the teaching process they can do best;
3. altering the size of the class so students will sometimes be in assembly classes, sometimes in inquiry classes, and sometimes in independent study;
4. assigning time to subjects according to their requirements for mastery, not according to the lockstep mold of a schedule which treats unequal subjects as equals.

The premise of IndiFlexS is: give the schools a flexible organization for teaching and good teachers can do an even better job than with a traditional school schedule.

If students of education study this plan and if administrators and teachers in the schools help to implement it, there is great promise for the quality of future American secondary education. Important as it is, the schedule is only the shell. With a new organization for learning, there is the mandatory implication that there will be new instructional techniques. Without adjustments in teaching methods, the full value of the schedule will fall short of its potential. Team teaching, increased use of technological aids, and new curricula can be utilized easily and effectively with IndiFlexS.

The genesis of this construct is not ours. It came from Dr. J. Lloyd Trump. Others may have added to it but he outlined it clearly in his provocative booklet, *Images of the Future*. Of course, he is not responsible for any flaws in this presentation. He gave the initial impetus to make the schools different and better. We are attempting to add fuel to Dr. Trump's fire with this guide to implementation.

The flexible scheduling concept has been employed in varying degrees by a large number of schools. Each has used some elements of the Trump concepts. This presentation draws on the experience of others as well as that of the authors. The procedures and the administrative steps suggested to construct IndiFlexS are based both on solid theory and practical experience.

### School Survey Included

Included in this discussion are the results of a survey of thirty-three schools (see Appendix One) using some form of flexible scheduling. It should be underscored that the schools surveyed are not the only ones using some variation of flexible scheduling. Also, of the schools included no two are probably using an identical organization. Only three of the schools are using all of the elements of IndiFlexS. Few have gone as far in their scheduling procedures as those outlined here, although most are moving in this direction. The informal survey was intended to be a basis of learning what schools are doing around the country, not an attempt to classify them.

The scheduling procedures advocated in this book are for a school wishing to become involved in a total flexible scheduled organization. While other plans, no doubt, will be proposed, this one is intended to be a model for further testing and evaluation. Care has been taken to include only those practices which have been successfully employed for at least three years in at least three school situations.

This process of schedule construction is only one approach. Better ways of actually constructing a flexible schedule may be developed later, but this procedure will get the task it is assigned to perform done now. No other claims should be made for it.

# Acknowledgments

GRATITUDE is due so many people who indirectly have been contributors to our efforts that we cannot possibly list them all.

We are indebted to colleagues who have patiently listened and constructively, yet helpfully, criticized our views and to students in colleges and administrators in high schools who have challenged these views with a friendly spirit. Particular acknowledgment is due J. Lloyd Trump. We are in his debt because of the vision he has provided in his writing and speaking and for his helpful criticism of this manuscript. What is written here is the authors' responsibility. Its faults should not reflect on the school we represent or our colleagues, but its strengths come to a large extent from them.

Special appreciation must be expressed to the administrators, interns, and teachers in the thirty-three schools which were surveyed for this book. Without their help in answering our exhaustive queries in a candid and complete way, much of the fiber of this book would be missing.

Careful attention was given to this manuscript by Miss Jane Rodman of the Indiana University Press. The authors were given a full measure of editorial and technical assistance from Miss Rodman.

Gratitude is due our families for their patience in our absence as the ideas presented here went from manuscript to book form.

D.C.M.

Bloomington, Indiana D.W.B.

# FLEXIBLE SCHEDULING

## Bold New Venture

# PART I

# FLEXIBLE SCHEDULING'S DYNAMIC POWER

## CHAPTER 1

# Flexible Scheduling for Quality Education

THESE ARE EXCITING TIMES to be working in the secondary schools. Long a Rip Van Winkle, American education is waking up. Dynamic new approaches to old problems are being proposed and tested. Curriculum reform is in the air. Modern mathematics, new approaches to science, increased emphasis on foreign languages, and readjustments of the social studies are practices no longer foreign to the public schools. Many new programs are in evidence. But new curricula alone are not enough to achieve the goal of quality education. Drastic changes are necessary in the methods used in instruction and in the way students learn. The full potential of the new curricula cannot be realized within the organizational framework of the conventional school. There is a need for the school to be organized to encourage students to be involved and active in the learning process, to allow teachers to meet with students for individual and small group discussions, and to vary the pace and the content of instruction for each student.

If the schools are to be significantly better, they must be substantially different. This view implies that a critical reexamination and searching appraisal of the organization for learning in each school be made. The newer media, modern learning theory, and flexible scheduling are aimed at individualizing instruction. The unifying motive for all efforts of educators must be to find workable ways to get from theory to practice in devising instruction appropriate for each individual. The traditional method of organizing the secondary schools, in which one teacher meets with five groups of approximately thirty students each day, will not do the job that needs to be done. The requirement of today's schools is to individualize and personalize instruction. Group teaching must give way to individual learning. Educators must stop dreaming about groups or classes and begin thinking of individuals or personalities. Group instruction should be used only as an aid to individual teaching. Far more emphasis and time in the school day must be given to the individual student than to group instruction.

The emphasis must be on the number one—one student with unique abilities, aspirations, and influencing experiences. At the same time, principals must not be thinking in terms of the faculty but in terms of each teacher, one at a time. The kind of education that society demands for our students is personal, unique, and supple. To make this a reality, principals must be aware of the distinct individual specialties and competence of every teacher. Teaching assignments must be varied to maximize the special abilities of every instructor.

Much has been written and said about individualized instruction. In the elementary school the educational system may have come the closest to this goal in reading instruction. At other levels of education, though, students have been frozen in rigid grade level or content groups and taught as if all students were one in ability and interest. As in the case of the weather, everyone talks but no one does anything about it. Unlike the weather, however, the school's condition can be influenced and improved. College professors have theorized, superintendents have generalized, principals have vocalized, and teachers have minimized the importance of providing for the individual differences of youngsters. At one time it was thought that unitary homogeneous grouping was the answer to the quest for quality instruction. With experience, disillusionment has grown regarding this crude technique.

What is said and what is done are at opposite ends of the continuum in terms of providing a unique educational experience for each student. Unequals are treated as equals when all students are given the same educational diet. Gifted students often are plunged into a pit of frustration as they are harnessed to a program that shackles their talents and restricts their creativity. Slow learners are sometimes stretched to the psychological breaking point as they, on the other hand, are asked to leap academic hurdles they cannot approach. To provide quality education the schools must personalize and individualize the instructional program. Educators should not waste a student's time on what he already knows or ignore the voids of understanding which inhibit his educational progress.

## What Quality Education Is

Good schools, in the context used here, are the ones with both concern and operational procedures to assist every youngster, irrespective of learning ability. There are no standardized tests devised that can measure a really fine school. Probably there never will be. The range of interests and the degrees of difference within a school population defy test measurement. The things tests measure—selected facts and restricted generalizations—are not the stuff of the quality school. Education is an affection for and an understanding of a process, not a body of multiple-choice questions. The goal of the school should be to instill a love of learning, to develop a thirst for inquiry, and to encourage a continual broadening interest in theoretical and practical affairs.

The good school sends a number of students to college, no nominal number however. Some schools serve areas in which the socioeconomic and ethnic complexion is such that college is not a sought-after value. Other schools exist almost essentially for college preparation. High school counselors sometimes have the difficult problem of helping some students understand that they should not go on for more formal education. Some students who are planning for college perhaps should be pursuing vocational preparation in the high school years.

America needs expert workers, whether in a research laboratory or on a production line. Good citizenship, with all it implies, is the national demand and a prized human value. The organization a school employs for instruction ought to be geared to every man's child. School experiences—discussing issues in a rational way; understanding the American heritage; and commanding the fundamental processes of reading, handling numbers, and communicating effectively —are the right of all. The school's organization for learning needs to give students opportunities for learning how to live productively as a result of rational thinking and action. For some students this may mean learning how to work in a retail store or in a food-service occupation. Human satisfaction comes from self-development at whatever the potential level an individual possesses. It is not necessarily measured by a college degree or a familiarity with Chaucer or Oppenheimer.

The good school is concerned with the slow learner, the emotionally or culturally deprived, as well as with the well-adjusted, the able and ambitious, and the economically secure youngster. The standard which makes a school excellent is measured by the indigenous characteristics of the particular school population. Comparison of standardized test norms or National Merit Scholarship winners is, at the very least, a dishonest judgment of how well a school meets its realistic challenges. The raw talent and the aspiration level of any school population is likely to be significantly different from neighboring schools. Family background, cultural advantage, and previous experiences vary from school area to school area. Each of these factors influences the lives of the students and should help shape the educational objectives of the school.

This is the moment for the schools to consider a better way of teaching, one that is in concert with the best of the learning practices. Flexible scheduling is suggested as an original way of helping all the children of all the people to develop their full capabilities and capacities. A flexible schedule is geared to the bright, the dull, the interested, and the disinterested. A flexible schedule is an approach to teaching and learning which stresses the teacher's professional judgment and the student's responsibility for his own learning.

### The Concept Defined

One of man's persisting problems is precise, effective communication. In education, as in other fields, the jargon plagues us. *Flexible* implies variability, pliability, fluidity; *schedule* implies uniformity, regularity, stability. The combination of flexible and schedule at the outset seems a gross contradiction. When we dig under the words and get to the meaning, however, a brilliant concept comes into focus. As used throughout this book, the flexible schedule is an organization for instruction which:

1. calls for classes of varying size within and between courses. (Students sometimes may meet in large assembly classes, and at other times in small inquiry classes. In addition, part of the day will be spent in individual or independent study.)
2. provides for instructional groups which meet at varying frequencies and for varying lengths. (Some classes may meet every day of the week, others will not. Some instructional sessions will be for a short duration, others for an extended period of time.)
3. makes team teaching possible in any content area or for any group of students in the school. (The use of a teaching team, two or more teachers working with a given group of students on a common instructional problem, is suggested in this model.)
4. requires countless professional decisions by teachers about students, content, and teaching methods.

The particular choice of options recommended in this discussion is referred to as IndiFlexS, the Indiana Flexible Schedule. IndiFlexS gives both a model and a procedure for implementing a flexible schedule. Not only is the theory of the flexible schedule presented, but the practical steps necessary to organize this operation are given.

### Size Set by Function

There are at least three kinds of general groups appropriate in IndiFlexS. First, there is a content presentation and testing group. This is usually a large group with up to three hundred students in it. Any activity in which the learner is involved in which he is quasi-active—listening to a lecture, filling in a learning program, viewing a film, or taking a test—can go on in a large assembly group, as well as in any other group size. While these groups are referred to as *large groups*, it is not their size but their function which is significant. It may be more appropriate to refer to these as *assembly groups* rather than large groups.

The second learning group is the one in which the student questions, discusses, clarifies, proposes, and uses his ideas and knowledge. Of necessity this group must be small, generally with only seven to fifteen students. Any more participants in this group would rob the individual of adequate opportunity to discuss and question. Perhaps there is good reason why no more than twelve are on a jury and why there were only twelve apostles. A group this size is manageable in discussion and free enough for questioning. While these groups have been popularly called *small groups,* it might be helpful to think of them as *inquiry groups.*

The third learning activity, and perhaps the most significant, is independent study. Usually independent study is the business of one person, although sometimes two or three work together profitably. This is an informal activity, not scheduled on a regular basis but open for the student to set and use as he sees fit.

The assembly and inquiry groups are scheduled. They are established by the faculty after careful judgments have been made about the nature of the course content and the students' requirements for mastery. The individual study time is open for the student to pursue whatever inquiry in whatever means he feels to be appropriate and productive. The purposes, means, and group sizes for each activity are summarized in Figure One.

### FLEXIBLE SCHEDULING PROCESSES

| Activity | Purpose and Function | Sample Means | Group Size |
|---|---|---|---|
| Independent or Individual Study | 1. Develop Skill or Assimilate Content | 1. Producing, Reading, Listening, Viewing | 1 |
| | 2. Reinforce Processes and Understandings | 2. Writing and Computing | 1 |
| | 3. Expand Areas of Interest | 3. Projects, Reports, Studies, Summaries | 1 |
| | 4. Broaden Background | 4. Reading, Listening, and Viewing | 1 |
| | 5. Formulate Interests and Learning Objectives | 5. Any Appropriate Means, Mostly Thought | 1 |
| | 6. Enlarge Capacity for Self-Development | 6. Committee Work, Discussion, and Listening | 1 or More |

| Activity | Purpose and Function | Sample Means | Group Size |
|---|---|---|---|
| | 7. Increase Knowledge Independent of Formal Instruction | 7. Study in any Appropriate Form | 1 or More |
| | 8. Refine Skills | 8. Activity in any Appropriate Form | 1 or More |
| | 9. Engage in Creative Thought | 9. Individual Activity in any Form | 1 |
| Inquiry or Small Groups | 10. Investigate General Problem Areas | 10. Group Interaction | 7-15 |
| | 11. Evaluate Ideas | 11. Discussion | 7-15 |
| | 12. Clarify Content Presentation and Understandings | 12. Questioning and Listening | 7-15 |
| | 13. Strengthen Listening and Speaking Skills | 13. Listening and Discussing | 7-15 |
| | 14. Sharing Experiences and Interpretations | 14. Panels, Buzz Groups, Discussion | 7-15 |
| | 15. Receive Specific Learning Help | 15. Teacher Prescriptions | 1 |
| | 16. Assume Leadership Responsibility | 16. Class Activity | 1 |
| Assembly or Large Groups | 17. Introduce Ideas, Present Knowledge | 17. Lecture with Visual Aids | 50-300 |
| | 18. Develop Background or Generalizations | 18. Lecture with Visual Aids | 50-300 |
| | 19. Test for Mastery | 19. Written Objective Tests | 50-300 |
| | 20. Enrich Instruction | 20. Recordings, Films, and any Other Appropriate Means | 50-300 |
| | 21. Summarize or Conclude Ideas | 21. Lecture with Visual Aids | 50-300 |

FIGURE ONE

*Traditional Schedule versus Flexible Schedule*

The traditional school schedule implies some assumptions that the use of a flexible schedule denies. While these are dealt with in detail throughout the book, it is appropriate to contrast some of them here.

| Element | Traditional Schedule | Flexible Schedule |
|---|---|---|
| Content | Assumes Each Course is equivalent in Requirements for Mastery to All Others | Assumes Requirements for Mastery of Content Vary from Course to Course |
| Facilities | Use is set by Schedule | Use is determined sometimes by Student Needs |
| Groups | All Class Groups are nearly Equal Size | Class Groups Differ in Size depending on the Instructional Task |
| Scheduling Unit | The Day; Each Day in the Week Has the Same Order as every other Day | The Week; Each Day in the Week Has Different Order |
| Students | Students Should Be in a Class Group or Supervised Study | Students May Be in a Class Group or Be Working Independently |
| Teachers | All Have Equal Numbers of Classes or Assignments and Demands on their Time | Number of Classes Vary from Teacher to Teacher and Demands on Time Vary |
| Time | Usually Equal for All Subjects | Usually Different for Various Subjects |

FIGURE TWO

The traditional organization for instruction is characterized by sameness. The order of each day is like the order of every other day. One teacher has a number of groups to meet similar in number to all teachers. One subject is studied for as long as all other subjects. One class meets for the same length of time as do all other classes.

It may be helpful in understanding the differences between the traditional and flexible schedule to visualize both. Figure Three represents a traditional school organization and Figure Four represents the IndiFlexS organization. In the models given, the length of the school day is the same. Both assume school begins at 8:30 A.M. and ends at 3:30 P.M. Each letter of the alphabet represents either a course or supervised study hall.

TRADITIONAL SCHEDULE WEEK

| Time | Monday | Tuesday | Wednesday | Thursday | Friday |
|------|--------|---------|-----------|----------|--------|
| 8:30 | A | A | A | A | A |
| 9:30 | B | B | B | B | B |
| 10:30 | C | C | C | C | C |
| 11:30 | L | U | N | C | H |
| 12:30 | D | D | D | D | D |
| 1:30 | E | E | E | E | E |
| 2:30 | F | F | F | F | F |

FIGURE THREE

The flexible schedule makes a very different set of assumptions from the timeworn organization. It is based on the view that each day's order need not be like any other day in the week. Teaching assignments have different demands and require various assignments of time. Group sizes vary according to the instructional technique used. The number of groups a teacher has is probably quite different from the number another teacher might have. Different subjects require different lengths of time and are best carried on in classes of various size. Classes with one set of purposes and complexities will meet for a different length and frequency than classes with other instructional purposes and complexities.

## INDIFLEXS WEEK

| Time | Monday | Tuesday | Wednesday | Thursday | Friday |
|---|---|---|---|---|---|
| 8:30 | A | E | A | B | A |
| 9:30 | B | | F | B | B |
| 10:30 | | A | | C | C |
| 11:30 | L | | | | F |
| 12:30 | C | U | N | A | H |
| 1:30 | F | D | C | | D |
| 2:30 | D | F | F / R | F | F |

FIGURE FOUR

In these models some of the differences are visualized. Course A in the traditional model has the same demands as all other courses. The group size is nearly always the same. Teachers can be expected to have at least one period for preparation and professional study. Students devote as much time to one course or activity as to another. F represents supervised study in Figure Three and independent study in Figure Four.

In the flexible model a student spends different amounts of time in course A than in other courses. This is not so in Figure Three. The longer-length classes are inquiry or small-group classes. The shorter-length classes are assembly or large-group classes. Independent study, of course, is represented by F. In this time a student fulfills his own learning objectives and is not a part of an organized group.

# CHAPTER 2

# Myths to Be Destroyed

Educators must unite to destroy the myths that are plaguing progress in achieving even better instructional programs. Somehow the fallacy that there are eternal laws about school organization has been allowed to go unchecked. A number of myths have been repeated so often that they are accepted without proper questioning. This folklore is an impediment to any school as it progresses toward individualizing instruction. On the one hand, to offer individualized instruction for every student is the stated goal. Then, to arrange students in rigid groups inhibits the realization of this noble and practical goal. The view that fundamental changes and fresh approaches to the teaching-learning process are necessary for meeting the real challenges of our age in education is fundamental in accepting the rationale for flexible scheduling. Five of these myths must be explored as the flexible scheduling concept is considered.

## Equal Time for Unequal Subjects

The first myth is the one that says all classes must meet for equal lengths of time. There is no research to validate this view and no experience to show that the length of all classes needs to be the same. As a matter of fact, repeated experience has established that it does not take as long to master some content as it does others. Yet educators continue to schedule all classes for equal lengths of time and usually for the same number of weekly meetings.

All courses are not the same in their conceptual depth or their educational benefit. In terms of time, it does not take as long to learn one subject as all others. It is a travesty on wisdom to continue to treat unequals as equals by insisting that all courses meet for the same length of time and as often each week. Educators must make particular decisions about the length of time a class should meet and the number of meetings which should be held for each course for each week. Students' welfare cannot be compromised for ease of administrative expediency. Of course, it is easier to schedule all courses for equal lengths of time, but it is neither professionally honest nor practically sound to do so.

Some classes can meet only two or three times a week and fulfill their objectives; others may require five or even more meetings per week. The number of meetings and the length of each meeting must be decided on the basis of the requirements for mastery by students. A school day is not a territory over which teachers battle, but the day is a territory for which a professional staff maps an efficient and successful procedure to help each student learn and understand.

### Accrediting Agencies and State Offices

A second myth comes from a widespread misunderstanding of the purposes of accrediting agencies and state departments of instruction. Often administrators say they cannot vary the length or frequency of class meetings, use team teaching, or other elements of IndiFlexS because of the restrictive requirements of accrediting agencies.

This is indeed a thin excuse. There is no section of the country in which some schools are not employing a flexible schedule, a violation of the unsound principle of equal time for unequal subjects. Accrediting agencies do give approval for flexible schedules if the reason is to improve instruction and if the school seeks the agency's permission to do so.

Accrediting associations are voluntary agencies legislated by the educators who manage the schools. What the educators order is what the accrediting agencies' policies will be. There was good reason for setting time requirements a generation ago. During the earlier periods (roughly from 1900-1940) school people needed these "requirements" to secure approval from boards of education for the staff necessary and to provide minimum resources for operating the schools. These policies were aids to pull the substandard schools up to acceptable staffing standards. The standards of ten to fifty years ago are not the same as those of today. Times have changed, so must the policies and standards which guide the school's operation.

There never has been a desire on the accrediting agencies' part to do anything but provide helpful policies for improving education. When the schools begin to recognize emerging needs, the agencies will be helpful companions in bringing about constructive new policies and standards.

If a flexible schedule is not to be employed, the reason for denying its use should be related to an instructional rationale and not to the thin excuse that accrediting agencies do not allow it. On the contrary, the fact is that accrediting agencies' leaders across the nation are encouraging experimentation and innovation.

In an address on evaluation at the 1964 Annual Meeting of the North Central Association of Colleges and Secondary Schools, Professor Donald C. Manlove of Indiana University urged schools to experiment with promising programs. Dr. Manlove said:

> Evaluation procedures can upgrade the program of the high school if encouragement is given to experimentation and to finding new and better methods of instruction. Procedures should provide for some uniformity desirable among schools and yet encourage and make provisions for the diversity essential to secondary schools attempting to provide for the needs of the school population they serve.

Propose a plan, develop a rationale, submit it to an accrediting agency, and see for yourself that it will be accepted. Instead of being scoffed at, you will probably end up on the program of the next annual meeting. Accrediting agencies want improved education. If flexible scheduling will achieve it, they will not stand in the way but applaud the innovators as positive steps toward development are taken.

A similar misconception sometimes exists about the attitude of state departments of instruction. Over the country state departments of education are giving approval and some, as in the case of Illinois, even are encouraging innovation and change in content, in teaching methods, and in scheduling procedures. By the assessment of some, New York is the state with the most indirect controls on the public schools, largely through the tradition of the Regents Examinations. Yet it is in New York that one can find some of the nation's finest models of flexible scheduling. State departments, by and large, are fulfilling a supervisory role. They have neither the personnel nor the function of encouraging innovation or program development in the schools. Usually they are constructive and helpful to educators who have a thoughtful plan to bring about better instruction. Few could be accused of inhibiting change and development of better organizations for learning.

However, a word of caution is in order. One cannot confuse the official judgment of either an accrediting agency or a state department with the off-the-cuff pronouncement of a representative of either group. Often it is lamentable that unknowing status people make unfounded judgments or generalized declarations. Another caution is given: the innovator should describe any program which deviates from the norm both to the accrediting officer and the state department official. They have the right and the responsibility to know what any school is doing. Not only will communication before the fact avoid misunderstanding or confusion, but often the agencies and their officers can be of help as the schools explore the frontiers of learning more about learning.

### It Will Not Work

A third myth that chokes change for the better in regard to flexible scheduling is the one that says simply, "It will not work." This has been proven false, yet it is recounted without seeking all the evidence. Because one man does not understand a concept or cannot easily develop operational procedures to implement an idea is no reason others cannot.

Examination of the programs of principals' meetings and workshops reveals a void in hearing anyone talk about the process of schedule construction. Since all administrators make a schedule one way or another, they do not usually pause long enough to consider new imaginative possibilities. There is considerable talk about a number of subjects over which educators have no control or influence, and at the same time there is neglect of the things that can be affected and altered. More conferences or sessions should be held to assess what is being done in organization for learning.

It is true that a flexible schedule requires more administrative time and effort than a relatively simple group schedule. The worth of the flexible schedule should outweigh the demands on both hours and work, however. If schools sincerely want to individualize learning, then they must be prepared to take the steps which make the goal a reality.

The purpose of IndiFlexS is to provide a set of orderly procedures whereby a school can work out a flexible schedule. There are other plans, some of more intricate detail, for getting the job done administratively. All of these approaches should be studied and evaluated, and then elements from each can be adapted for an individual school's use.

There are many things a principal cannot control. He cannot usually alter the financial picture of the schools or create new facilities. He cannot control the sociological climate of the school. However, he can have a significant influence on the school by the decisions he makes and the work he does in the school's schedule and organization for learning.

Perhaps one of the most important functions a principal fulfills is constructing the school schedule. As he does this, he orders a student's day, he deploys a teacher's talent, and he establishes the climate for learning. The school schedule establishes the means by which its instructional ends can be adequately achieved.

Only a principal who knows his staff and who has a clear idea about the purposes of a secondary school can hope to be a positive force in the school. The school schedule is the evidence of this knowledge. The master schedule is the vehicle for activating what the principal believes about student needs and teacher capabilities. The schedule construction, while the principal's responsibility ultimately, is the combined business of the teaching and administering staffs. The teachers recommend and the administrators mediate and facilitate.

## Change Does Not Always Cost More Money

A fourth myth haunting public school educators is the one that says that any changes will cost more money. This must be identified as a major roadblock to progress in education. Maybe schools do need more professional people, more facilities, more materials, and more, more of everything else. These needs do not arise just because a flexible schedule is employed. If educators show by effort and creative proposals that the schools are changing, adapting, and trying to improve, the *more* of everything will come easier. There is also the possibility that, as the schools organize in new ways, they will not have the same needs we imagine now. Improvement can come by change through substitution as well as change through addition. The schools can reduce the number of costly certified teachers by increasing the number of less expensive paraprofessional staff members. Machines can do some things, for less money, that humans do. In many instances, all of this adds up to a decrease in per pupil expense.

Any school facility which can operate a traditional schedule can accommodate a flexible schedule. True, it would be nice to have new facilities for new programs. For that matter, it is pleasant to have new facilities for old programs. Too often educators think about past practices of methodology when they think of future building needs. Wise administrators, to the contrary, will plan new structures so future programs of organization will fit easily and appropriately into these new spaces. While some facilities eliminate some kinds of flexibility, no school building makes all features of IndiFlexS impossible.

A school does not need to add more staff necessarily because of a flexible schedule. As a matter of fact, the claim has been made by some that they need fewer staff with the flexible schedule. When one establishes a motive, almost any rationalization can be used in its name! An analysis of the contention that flexible scheduling saves money per se, though, proves false. Schools that reduce their staff needs because of a flexible schedule could have done the same thing with a traditional schedule if staff reduction was the only goal. That is, the staff size is also determined by intent and other factors and not by organization for instruction alone.

IndiFlexS has as one of its aims an increased amount of time for teacher preparation and study. To increase the amount of preparation time costs money if class size and independent study time are not taken into consideration. The point is: an administrator can do anything with the schedule, reduce teacher needs or increase them. The principle of flexible scheduling does neither by itself. Instead, it is a new way of deploying whatever resources are at hand.

## Teachers Do Not Want Change

In the discussion of myths, perhaps the most devastating one supplies educators with an excuse for not thinking, planning, and acting. It goes like this: "I, as principal, would like to inaugurate a flexible schedule but my staff does not want differences between schedules in this school and surrounding schools. They are conservatives."

What is a conservative teacher anyway? Is it one who does not want the best for his students? Is it one who denies progress and is afraid of new ideas? Too often principals and teachers are asked or, more often, decide to make decisions without all the facts and a complete understanding of what they are asked to do. Educators need to study the implications of a traditional schedule. Likewise, a faculty needs to be aware of all the implications and the specific values implied in flexible scheduling before attempting to employ the concept. Flexible scheduling implies a way of teaching different from the traditional situation. The flexible schedule is more than a game of time and group size redistribution.

Teachers must have the whole picture of a flexible schedule before they are asked to make a judgment about it. They need to understand its rationale, see how they fit into the local plan, and know what the implications are for their teaching behavior. The survey done as IndiFlexS was developed revealed a serious and long-range talking partnership between the principal and the staff in schools using a flexible scheduling program. Administrators who give real leadership are those who have a planned in-service program and who are not satisfied with simple pronouncements about complex problems.

## The Principal's Role

These myths can only be put to rest with information and inquiry. The principal makes the difference in any school as to whether accurate data and real understandings exist or whether myths pass as truths.

In each flexible scheduled school the authors have studied, it is significant that the building principal played an important role in working with the staff in developing new teaching procedures. The principal must give positive support and overt educational leadership to the staff if the flexible schedule is to hit its target of improving instruction.

The building principal is necessarily the key figure in raising significant questions about the teaching procedures and organization used in a school. Questioning and searching for better ways to teach are not signs of local disloyalty but marks of honest professional initiative. The principal's central responsibility is to help the faculty improve the school's instructional program. If he does not ask the right questions, the wrong answers and inadequate programs should be a surprise to no one. For instance, if a question is raised about research not validating the use of a flexible schedule, the principal needs to respond with an answer that points out there are some answers research cannot give. Further, he needs to explain why this is so. He needs to have the reference data at his finger tips.

It is the principal who makes the difference also between adequate and superior education in any school. This is stated not to diminish the teacher's role, but to say that no teacher's full potential can be released unless an effective leader opens doors of understanding and provides the opportunity for teachers to teach in the grand manner. The teacher influences what does or does not happen in a classroom. The principal, on the other hand, has a universe of influence which extends throughout the school. The principal is the teachers' teacher. It is his job to present ideas, to discuss alternate courses of action, and to help others see that different alternatives may be fruitful.

CHAPTER *3*

# Instruction by Involvement and Design

W<small>HEN THE EDUCATOR</small> constructs the school's master schedule he is arranging precious units—teaching talent, content, student learning needs, time, and facilities—in a manner which may or may not be complementary. The way these units are brought together can have a profound effect on both the quality of teaching and learning which goes on in a school. The job of the one who finally constructs the master schedule is to arrange valuable teaching time so that it is potentially possible to use it in the most effective manner. At the same time, the schedule should place students in learning situations that are at once personally rewarding and educationally productive. This kind of schedule construction demands careful analysis of the teachers' competencies and the students' instructional requirements. The principal who constructs an IndiFlexS program makes judgments each time he orders an element in the schedule.

The school's schedule should be structured by a series of decisions, not by happenstance. Too often the schedule is constructed by expediency and not by careful design. Scheduling students is a time-consuming task once the master schedule itself is set. It is not wise, however, to ignore the potential for advantage to students in the pressure to get done the huge clerical job of making class lists, balancing sections, and attempting to avoid conflicts of two courses a student wants being offered at the same time.

The effort of scheduling frequently is relegated exclusively to a summer's responsibility of the administrator. If scheduling is to be done in an effective way, it must be a cooperative endeavor between the teaching staff and the administrators. Before a decision is made and cemented in a schedule, alternate options should be discussed and evaluated. Frequently, schedule construction procedures are restricted to adjustments of the previous year's schedule. Creative new arrangements of time and talent are not considered because the assumption is made that last year's schedule was the ideal from which next year's schedule will be made.

The usual method of constructing a schedule is to begin by assigning teachers to periods in the day in which their instruction is to be given. This can put *ipso facto* restrictions on what students can take, on grouping potentials, and on team teaching meetings during the school day. The IndiFlexS sequence begins by assessing student elections, determining the best possible specifications of learning groups, and then generating the master schedule.

### How Much Time Does It Take?

Estimating the time it takes to generate IndiFlexS is folly. There are too many uncontrolled variables. Some principals work at lightning speed. Others do not. Some schools have difficult space limitations and others are free from this restriction. The sheer size of the school also adds to the difficulty in determining the length of time it takes to schedule a school.

Contrary to a popular notion, it may take appreciably longer to construct a flexible schedule for a school of three hundred than a much larger school. The larger school has more sections and more facilities and, thus, more opportunity for easy movement and adjustment.

The question is not so much related to the amount of time it takes, but more to the point is: Will a flexible schedule be worth the effort? Will individualizing instruction be sufficient reward for this increased expenditure of time and energy it takes for scheduling?

It should be pointed out forcefully that a flexible schedule, with or without data processing, will take considerably longer to create than a traditional schedule. Also, IndiFlexS requires the cooperation and participation of the total teaching staff. To believe otherwise would be an unfortunate and erroneous notion.

## Working With the Staff

The administrator who constructs the master schedule without the consultation and recommendations of the teaching staff is probably saving himself a great amount of time but, at the same time, he is ignoring a rich pool of ideas that can contribute to a superior schedule. Teachers are likely to make suggestions which reflect their professional strengths. When a teacher suggests that he work with a given group of students or concentrate on one teaching role, there is every likelihood that will be the teacher's strength. It usually follows that people are good at what they like and want to do; conversely, they are not as good at doing what they neither like nor want to do. The principal should be the broker between teachers' preferences and performances.

The business of schedule construction is a cooperative enterprise when it reaches its fullest fruition. The conversations about what is to be taught and how it is to be approached should go on after the student instructional needs are understood by the faculty. The guidance counselors can supply the teaching faculty with information about the student body learned from individual conferences with students and from standardized test results. What a pity it is when the accumulation of significant test data is allowed to stay buried in a file cabinet when this information could be beneficial to the staff as decisions are made about teaching and learning arrangements. Test data has as much value for the staff as it has for the students. The value is on very different levels but both can serve ultimate pupil advantage if used properly.

Throughout this discussion recurrent references will be made to the guidance counselors. Both the number of references and the importance of the functions assigned to counselors indicate the importance of staff members within the modern secondary school. The IndiFlexS model places added responsibilities on the counselors. The philosophical and operational orientation of some counselors is hostile, it is recognized, to the role described throughout this discussion. Happily this is not always the case. Many counselors do see their role as one intertwined with the teaching and administrative staff as decisions are made about what is taught and how it is taught. The counselor can be a helpful partner in the curricular decisions made in the school. His particular knowledge of and familiarity with students puts him in a position to make special contributions to discussions about what students need to study and, more important perhaps, how they feel about the school's program.

The counselors should also be charged with the responsibility of getting the course elections from the students. In addition, the counselors will consult with the teachers as they establish the specifications for membership in the various learning groups. The determination of learning-group specifications will be discussed later in detail. When the counselors do not perform these services, someone else needs to do it or the considerations that should go into the schedule construction will fall below their full potential.

Each school that goes into a flexible schedule needs to make certain that the roles and responsibilities of the staff are defined. Without a clear understanding of who is to decide what, the decisions will necessarily be left to the principal and his assistant principal or be settled by inclination rather than design.

Working on the schedule is a valuable in-service education activity. It is amazing how much thinking, discussing, and reading teachers do as they become immersed in schedule-construction considerations. Some decisions are for the faculty as a whole, some are the concern of departments, and still others will fall in the province of consideration of the teaching teams or individual teachers. Department meetings, faculty meetings, and special conferences will be needed as the schedule is developed to zero-in on the many alternate options available for organizing for learning.

### An All-Year Job

Constructing the master schedule is an all-year job. It cannot be relegated to brief consideration if it is to seek its level of providing the best opportunity for youngsters to learn. Few other, if any, considerations are as important as the construction of the school's schedule for a staff. Since the schedule puts the fence around what teachers and students can and cannot do in the formal school day, it should be discussed in detail, element by element.

It is suggested that each year the staff review their educational objectives. Penetrating questions should be asked to find out if the courses or learning activities and the school's policies are in concert with the institution's objectives as the years go by. It is expected that the school's objectives will change. Society is not static. The school should not be unchanging; it should be continually adjusting to the needs of the student body as they are modified. Students from one section of the same community may very well have a need for a different emphasis in instruction than students from another part of the same community. These differences should be assessed by the faculty and the school policies and activities adjusted to suit them.

A common objective of many schools is "to provide educational opportunities for all students." Alarming dropout rates, few graduates attending college, high failure percentages, and disinterest in school activities often show this noble objective is not being met. The school either needs to change the objective to state the school exists for students with only certain specific scholastic abilities and interests or it needs to change its policies and content of some courses. It is a fascinating experience to contrast many schools' stated objectives with their operational practices.

Once the faculty has settled on the immediate school objectives, it is time to begin selecting means to achieve these goals. This is where the considerations of curriculum should properly begin. The guidance counselors can contribute much to this consideration as they assess and report on the particular characteristics of the student body.

Schools have had a tendency to increase the requirements for graduation in the senior high school years over the last decade. Sputnik, increased need for education as a requirement for employment, and a more literate society have all contributed to this addition of requirements. This may be an unfortunate trend. All students are not benefited by conforming to a single standard. For some the standard will fall short of the potential a school could ask of a student; for others it will be an unrealistic, impossible demand. It may be all right to require four years of English for graduation, for example, but the content of the four-year sequence should not be the same for all students.

When requirements are set universally, they should not have time requirements pinned to them. For example, some youngsters may profit greatly from only three hours of English instruction a week and two hours of something else, while still others may need more than five hours of instruction in English to accomplish their needs. Of course, deviations of this kind from traditional practice need to be carefully thought out and approved by the local school board, the state department of public instruction, and the regional accrediting agency before implementation. As the educational profession continues to grow in knowledge, skill, and popular respect, changes from universal requirements to individual requirements will become the norm. This means that the decision-making competency of the educator will be called into play more often and his judgment will necessarily be more formally recognized.

After the instructional objectives are identified and the content is selected to meet these objectives, the means by which the instruction is to take place must be determined. IndiFlexS calls for three general kinds of learning groups—independent study, inquiry group, and assembly group—as was explained in Chapter 1.

This is not to imply that only these three kinds can be called for, but these are the basic groups that a school using IndiFlexS will want to use. Some activities, like laboratory sessions, may be as profitable with thirty students in them as with seven to fifteen. The group size is determined by the teachers as they consider the learning activities to be engaged in. Unnecessary restraint is put on the concept of flexible group size when the limits are set automatically without reason. It does no good to exchange one set of orthodoxies for another.

### Decisions for Each Course

For each course the school offers the faculty must make decisions about the size of each learning group, the frequency of learning-group meetings, and the duration of each learning activity. As has been indicated, the size of the group is determined by the method of instruction to be used. Teacher-centered activities call for assembly groups; student-centered activities call for inquiry groups. If the method of instruction is to be mainly by teacher lectures, then there will be a correspondingly large number of assembly groups. When the method of instruction lays emphasis on discussion and pupil interaction, there will necessarily be increased numbers of inquiry groups. Before decisions can be made about the method of instruction to be used, the teachers have to have specific ideas about the content of their courses and about the particular characteristics of the student body.

Not only the size but also the frequency of class meetings needs to be set. Some classes may meet daily, others will meet less often. When the frequency of meetings is considered, the length of duration of each meeting should be taken into consideration.

## Limited Lecture Sessions

IndiFlexS calls for assembly groups that are thirty minutes in length. Students usually can assimilate what is presented in this period of time much better than in lengthy listening sessions. For secondary school youngsters, a longer teacher presentation is likely to result in some daydreaming, pencil-tapping, and other escape mechanisms. If it takes more than one listening session of thirty minutes a day for a student to understand a concept, then the student may need an individual conference with a teacher.

## Modules Are Building Blocks

The IndiFlexS day is divided into modules of time. Each module is thirty minutes long. There are fifteen modules in the day. This corresponds to a seven-period day with a half-hour lunch period. The length of the module is determined by the shortest learning activity— the assembly group—in the school day. The inquiry group is constructed by connecting modules. For instance, if an inquiry group is to be an hour and a half in length, then three modules are connected to get the desired length.

Both the frequency and the duration of class meetings are set by the instructional tasks the teacher establishes for them. Thus, all courses will not meet for equal lengths or total amounts of time. Instead, group meetings will be set by the instructional requirements of the group.

Also, teaching assignments will vary. Those teachers who make assembly group presentations will need more time for preparation than those who work with the inquiry groups since it is not possible to prepare for an inquiry group as it is for an assembly group.

The questions, the problems, the clarifications a teacher is called upon to give in the inquiry group are determined on the spot and depend on the student's understandings or lack of them. However, the well-constructed, clear expositions necessary for the assembly-group presentations take time to prepare. Time should be provided in the school day for these presentation preparations. Because study and preparation are important prerequisites to good teaching, these professional activities should not be relegated to after hours' work but should be a part of the teacher's school day.

Since team teaching requires that teachers meet to consult, to exchange ideas, and to make decisions, this too should be part of the school day's professional activity. Some teams will need to meet more often than others but a minimum number of team-planning sessions should be established for each team. As the schedule is constructed, specific times should be set aside for team meetings during the regular school day.

### The Schedule Cycle

IndiFlexS calls for a schedule cycle that is based on the week. In most schools the schedule cycle is the day. Each day the schedule is the same as every other day. Monday's class schedule is like Tuesday's and every other day in the week. IndiFlexS programs dictate for teachers and students that every day in the week might, and probably will, call for a schedule different from every other day in the week although the schedule will repeat itself each week. Figure Three and Figure Four should be studied again to see the difference in the cycle. The weekly cycle allows for longer periods of study, unequal distributions of time for various courses, and gives latitude in organizing special groups to meet one, two, three, or four times a week without having to meet five times a week for equal lengths of time. Some courses can have activities which may meet twice during one day or not at all for a particular day.

The cycle can be a two-day or three-day arrangement, as well as a single day or week. The longer the cycle, the more opportunity there is for varying the patterns of organization of learning groups. The selection of the week as the cycle was made so that teachers could choose from a wide range in distribution of time and frequencies of class meetings. Using the week as the cycle, teachers think in terms of five days when making decisions about the size, the number, and the duration of learning groups.

Experience has shown that students respond favorably to the variability of the week cycle. There is adventure and freshness to the week cycle of classes that is not to be found in the traditional schedule. Sometimes when people are introduced to the idea of a week's scheduling cycle, there is apprehension that students will forget their schedules, that they will be bothered by the lack of daily repetition of classes, and that a loss will result in retention of facts and ideas with the irregularity of class meetings. Experience has shown these are unfounded fears. Students at the Brookhurst Junior High School in Anaheim, California, have schedule changes on a weekly basis and adjust well to this practice. While the Brookhurst schedule is not on a cycle as advocated in IndiFlexS, this experience does substantiate the claim, verified elsewhere as well, that students operate profitably with an extended cycle.

### Facilities Play a Part

Facilities need to be considered as the schedule is constructed. They sometimes place restrictions on the arrangements teachers feel is best for a given group of students. However, an unfortunate tendency exists which illogically assigns faults to facilities. Any school that has the space to house a traditional schedule has the space to accommodate IndiFlexS. There may be limited restrictions on large-group areas, but often these can be overcome with imagination and reusing some spaces. The problem of facilities is discussed in more detail in Chapter 6. It is an unreasoning public that does not expect changes to be made inside school buildings. We do not live in the same kinds of houses as we did a quarter of a century ago, and we cannot expect a wall of mortar and brick to stand in the way of improved instruction. Remodeling and redeployment of space within a school should be considered by every school administrator from time to time.

As the schedule is constructed, the availability of facilities and specialized equipment needs to be taken into account. This should be

done by mimeographing a form which lists the various specialized spaces on one axis and the modules on another. This form
should be given to the departments at an early stage of schedule consideration.

## With Whom Shall They Learn

Serious consideration needs to be given to the group specifications set
for each class group. There is an advantage for the teachers and for
students in particularistic grouping for specific classes. For teachers
it helpfully limits their range of considerations and for students it
creates a comfortable and potentially meaningful atmosphere for free
inquiry.

Group specifications should be set for every learning group in the
school. It may be that the final decision will be to group some classes
or even most on a random basis. Still it is wise to come to this decision
after consideration of the alternatives. And after several years' experience with IndiFlexS, it is doubtful that a faculty will come to this con-
clusion. Experience has shown that, as schools have used a flexible
schedule for several years, more specially organized sections are
formed. Inquiry groups are often organized according to particularistic specifications.

The number of ways to group students for instruction is almost infinite. Teachers can set up inquiry-group specifications based on
chronological age, sex, achievement in reading, computation or any
other intellectual ability, personality characteristics, behavior patterns, skill mastery, ethnic background, stated vocational choice or
interest. The limits of the group specifications are the teaching procedures of the teachers and the measures of the characteristics to be
grouped.

The sole purpose of any grouping is to establish an atmosphere in
which optimum learning can take place. Sometimes teachers can provide for individual differences better when the span of difference is
reduced within a group. Also, students of common interest and pro-
ficiency are frequently stimulated while feeling secure in a group of
students of similar characteristics.

Educators have become disenchanted with grouping practices

when a student is grouped for all subjects by a single criterion. For example, an intelligence quotient score is an invalid index for grouping youngsters in all classes. An individual can have a high I.Q. score and, at the same time, have a deficient ability or lagging interest in one subject. Unfortunately this was not recognized when homogeneous grouping came into vogue in the 1930's.

Some grouping is done so that the instruction, either in its depth or breadth or both, can be varied by the teacher. This allows the group to consider ideas on a level appropriate to the understanding of the learner. On the other hand, grouping is sometimes organized because the teacher wants a group of students to establish a particular cohesiveness for a specific purpose, as in the case of grouping done by certain behavior characteristics. One English teacher grouped all the shy, retiring female students in a group. The purpose was to provide an atmosphere where able but retiring youngsters could gain security difficult for them to find in other groups. The successes reported were legion.

While grouping based on past school performance in a subject is by far the most frequently used, other kinds of groupings offer great promise for increasing the learning potential of students. Because of the size of inquiry groups, from seven to fifteen students, and because of the large number needed for most every course, the practicability of actually arranging these groups is increased considerably.

The assembly groups often will be heterogeneous groups, although it is not uncommon to have several tracks or levels of instruction in a school of over six hundred pupils. The grouping for the assembly classes is necessarily wider in range of abilities or characteristics than in the smaller inquiry groups. Once again, the question must be asked: What is the best arrangement of students to achieve the stated ideas of instruction? The guidance counselors can be of inestimable assistance in helping decide who should be in various groups established by the teachers.

### But Not Least

The final area of consideration, but definitely not the least important, is the professional staff. It has been found advantageous to delay the assignment of teaching staff until after the matters mentioned earlier have been settled. All teachers may be more active in the previously mentioned study of topics if the teaching assignments are not settled first. Also, the study of the objectives, content, methods of instruction, and numbers of classes helps teachers determine what aspects of the teaching process they want to perform.

## Teaching Teams and Nonprofessional Aides

Teaching in a flexible schedule calls upon teachers to work together on teaching teams or by cooperative teaching. Take your pick of the labels. It is difficult for some teachers to be part-time team members if they are really going to count in this new role. Faculty meetings, workshops, and other in-service activities are a part of the early stage of a flexible scheduled school. The role of team teaching is discussed in more detail in Chapter 5.

The use of nonprofessional aides to teachers has been talked about more than used. Those few schools in the country who do use noncertified helpers for teachers as a part of the regular staff report positive reactions to the aides. While some school districts use noncertified personnel as members of the teams, this option is not an essential part for the use of IndiFlexS, even though it is recommended.

Noncertified school workers can have an important place in fulfilling supportive tasks for the teaching staff. Locating information, typing resource materials, correcting some papers, making visuals, and performing countless other services for the teaching staff are some of the functions these adjuncts to the professional staff can perform. In the IndiFlexS model the service personnel are assigned to specialized functions and work for any teacher in the school. One noncertified aide would work on audiovisual aids, another would work as a typist— sometimes taking material from voice-recording equipment—and the other members of the noncertified staff would have different particular operations to perform. The noncertified aides would work out of one area and give their service on the *ad hoc* basis to each of the teams or teachers in the school.

In summary, the sequence of topics for decisions to be made is given in Figure Five.

DECISION-MAKING CONSIDERATIONS

| Sequence | Topic | Time-Suggestion |
|----------|-------|-----------------|
| First | School Objectives | September-October |
| Second | Content Selection | November-December |
| Third | Education Requirement Determination | January |
| Fourth | Learning Group Size, Frequency and Duration Determination | January-March |
| Fifth | Schedule Cycle—Specifics for Each Course | March |
| Sixth | Facility Use (Essentially by Administrators) | March |
| Seventh | Group Specifications—Faculty Consults Counselors | April |
| Eighth | Team Teaching Assignments | April |
| Ninth | Noncertified Staff Requirements | April |
| Tenth | Final Student Elections | May |

FIGURE FIVE

## Student Elections

Final student elections should be assembled by the guidance staff late in the school year. Students should give the counselors their tentative vocational goals as well as parent-approved course elections for the next year.

## IndiFlexS Preferences

Figure Six gives the IndiFlexS preferences and some of the alternate options for each of the scheduling elements. Within each of these dimensions, there are both arrangement and matching decisions which need to be made. The element of content must be selected or put in sequence. The distribution of class sizes, length and frequency of meeting, grouping criteria, and facility use must be arranged. The sequence for arranging these elements in the schedule will be discussed in subsequent chapters.

SCHEDULING ELEMENTS

| Dimension | IndiFlexS Preference | Alternatives |
|---|---|---|
| Content | x | 1. Unitary subject areas with defined content<br>2. Unitary subject areas with undefined content<br>3. Coordination of more than one subject area with defined content<br>4. Coordination of more than one subject area with undefined content |
| Students | x | 1. Learn in equally balanced groups<br>2. Learn in varying class-sized groups |
| Period Length | x | 1. Every period is equal in length<br>2. Multiple periods for some courses<br>3. Period length preset in terms of class sizes and instructional functions<br>4. Period length determined by teachers within an assigned block for one or more subjects<br>5. No assigned period length made |
| Time | x | 1. Standard distribution of time for all subjects<br>2. Standard distribution of time but varies by grade levels<br>3. Various distributions of time for each subject<br>4. Distribution of time varies; established on *ad hoc* basis |
| Cycle | x | 1. One day<br>2. Two days<br>3. One week<br>4. Not set; determined on an *ad hoc* basis |
| Instructional Media | x | 1. Media used on an *ad hoc* basis<br>2. Planned use of media in an established order<br>3. Media used as part of individual study |

| Facilities | | |
|---|---|---|
| | x | 1. Multi-purpose facilities<br>2. Highly specialized facilities<br>3. Semi-specialized facilities |
| Teachers | x | 1. One teacher working with a given number of students in equally balanced groups<br>2. One teacher working with a given number of students in varying class-sized groups<br>3. A team of teachers (two or more) working with a given number of students in equally balanced groups<br>4. A team of teachers working with a given number of students in varying class-sized groups |
| Noncertified Instructional Aides | x | 1. Members of teaching teams<br>2. Service personnel who assist on an *ad hoc* basis |

FIGURE SIX

PART II

INFLUENCES OF FLEXIBLE SCHEDULING

CHAPTER 4

# Students and Flexible Scheduling

Experience has shown that a flexible schedule can be accepted by students, sometimes even with unbounded enthusiasm. Youngsters like the variety that a flexible schedule offers, and they react positively toward the opportunity for activity it provides. In a flexible schedule there is less likelihood of humdrum boredom since every day's activities are not like those of other days. There is a natural adolescent affection for the variability of the new schedule when it allows them to work on projects on their interest level. Each day becomes special, and every class is apt to claim more student attention in the flexible schedule than in the production-type organization of a traditional schedule. The value of the flexible schedule cannot be realized if students do not work and operate in new and different ways. Emphasis for the student is on action. The learner reads, discusses, writes, constructs, and is highly involved in the learning process, to a degree not customary in a traditional class organization.

Students easily learn to get in the correct place at the right time under such an organization, contrary to the fears of some experienced educators. It is folly to assume that even the dullest student cannot find the proper class in a flexible schedule. When effective large-group presentations are to be given, students anticipate them in a positive fashion. They look forward to the small group where they can discuss ideas and challenge their own ability to communicate. They enjoy independent study when it provides the opportunity to work on problems at their own rate of progress. When organized around topics of concern to the learner, reading and writing are much more pleasant.

If the flexible schedule meets its aim of inceased quality of instruction, students will respond with positive voluntary reaction toward school. When laboratory classes are extended for several hours, students get a sense of satisfaction from completing their work to a degree not possible in the usual fifty-minute period. For example, they actually like to see a picture design completed in one three-hour period. In homemaking they can go through all the steps at one time in the process of preparing a meal. Unity can be given to learning activities in a way that the shorter periods will never allow. Through this unity real insights can be developed that are fragmented in the shorter class sessions.

## The Student's Schedule

It is impossible to present a universal model schedule for a student in IndiFlexS since each student's schedule is likely to be different from every other student's in the school. IndiFlexS calls for each student's program to be tailor-made to the particular educational needs and aspirations a youngster has. The schedules of a number of students may tend to look alike in the early stages of the use of Indi-FlexS. As the years go by, the variations will naturally become more pronounced.

In the early stages of the use of IndiFlexS there may be good reason to schedule more assembly and inquiry classes in each subject than will be scheduled after IndiFlexS has been used for several semesters. Students need to be given help in the techniques of independent self-assumed study, as well as the motivation to do it. Most of the student's previous school experience has been dominated by teacher determination of what a student studies, how he approaches the content or skill, why he explores the topic or topics, and when he does much of his work. IndiFlexS revises all this. Each student works at his own rate on topics which may be teacher-assigned but often are student-assumed. Great latitude is available for determining when a student works on a particular topic. Students will use a variety of methods for study in IndiFlexS; each calls for his own active effort in thinking, reading, writing, constructing, and so forth.

The students in grades seven and eight are likely to require more time in assembly groups than the students in grades eleven and twelve. The total distribution of time for students in assembly and inquiry groups and independent study in grades seven through twelve is suggested in Figure Seven in terms of the work week of about thirty-six hours of school instruction, excluding lunch hours and homeroom periods.

APPROXIMATE WEEKLY TIME DISTRIBUTION—GRADES SEVEN
THROUGH TWELVE

| Year in School | Assembly Group | Inquiry Group | Independent Study |
|---|---|---|---|
| 7 | 55% or 19½ hours | 30% or 10½ hours | 15% or 5¼ hours |
| 8 | 50% or 18 hours | 35% or 12½ hours | 15% or 5¼ hours |
| 9 | 50% or 18 hours | 35% or 12½ hours | 15% or 5¼ hours |
| 10 | 45% or 16¼ hours | 30% or 10½ hours | 25% or 9 hours |
| 11 | 40% or 14¼ hours | 30% or 10½ hours | 30% or 10½ hours |
| 12 | 30% or 10½ hours | 30% or 10½ hours | 40% or 14¼ hours |

FIGURE SEVEN

## Is Flexible Scheduling for all Students?

As educators are introduced to this new concept of organizing for learning a common question pops up. Teachers want to know if flexible scheduling is an advantage to all students. Fear is expressed by some that it might not have advantage to all students; some are apprehensive that it might not have advantage for the gifted; others express the same concern for the scholastically disinclined or disadvantaged. Interestingly enough, the concern teachers have is not centered on either group. Reasons are advanced by some as to why the slow learner cannot adjust to the proposed new patterns. Other faculty members deny these potential dangers and verbalize concern for the rapid learner. They contend the gifted student needs a class meeting on a sustained daily basis to hear a teacher's lecture so the student can learn big bulks of information. Once again, experience has a lesson. A flexible schedule holds no particular disadvantage to either group, the slow or gifted students. Both groups of students appear to fit into the new patterns equally well.

The relatively small group of students who express dissatisfaction with the flexible schedule initially are not to be found in significant numbers among either the able groups or the disadvantaged learning groups. The distribution of students expressing dissatisfaction are to be found among students of various abilities, according to a survey made of the students at University Junior High School in Bloomington, Indiana. This survey found that students of all ability levels found they liked large-group sessions the least, independent study was rated next, and small-group instruction got the highest rating from these junior high school students. This preference trend was noted among students of both high and low ability and interest in school. The flexible schedule is not the end of the rainbow for all students, but it is apparently an alternative with promise for doing a better job of joining ideas, teachers, and time with students in a profitable union.

## Advantages to Students

A flexible schedule allows a student to spend time on educational activities which are of interest and concern to him. From this foundation of interest solid understandings can be built.

The flexible schedule gives a student the opportunity to get personal attention and direction from a teacher. The organizational arrangement puts teachers in contact with students in a one-to-one relationship. This requires a different kind of approach to teaching. When the student comes to the teacher, it is more often with his problem or question. The teacher who helps students in independent study or meets with the student in the small group is an adviser and a helper. The role of teller and dictator vanishes, and a new role for the teacher emerges. Students reply in a positive fashion to a warm responsive teacher. The same motive that prompts the youngster to say "Look at me, Dad," as he goes off the diving board prompts him to want to show his teacher his best work.

Changing the organization for instruction brings about a new image which students develop about their learning and their teacher. Learning becomes a personal quest, and a sense of mission develops as a youngster attacks problems in his area of interest. The teacher is received as a source of help, as a fellow voyager to understanding. As a staff goes into flexible schedule, it needs to concentrate its efforts on creating a new climate in the school. This is characterized by friendly permissiveness, yet it has control through firm expectations for each student to work, to read, to write, and to construct.

One student, Richard Gold, at the Meadowbrook Junior High School, Newton, Massachusetts, summarized this new kind of teacher in this way:

> "Before I was on a flexible schedule the teachers asked us most of the questions. Now the situation is reversed. It is the students who are questioning the teachers. I have worked harder and done more work in school since we have been on the flexible schedule than ever before. Now it is fun to work in school. It does not seem like school work!"

## The Extension of the Principle

Almost every educator, regardless of stature and recognized ability, worships at the altar of individual differences. Educators recognize students are different in size, interest, experience, and almost every other imaginable way. Yet when teachers get to the classroom, they ask everyone to do the same assignment, and turn it in on the same day; and then they evaluate it by the same standard.

As teachers go into a flexible schedule, they must recognize the difference in learners and want to provide for them individually in various ways. This means that the larger the group of students in a flexible schedule, the greater the differences will be between the members of the groups in capability and interest. That is, disparity in the group's accomplishment and understanding is the goal of the flexible schedule.

The span of the curriculum should widen in the flexible schedule. Instead of all students reading one novel in an English class, it will be possible for one hundred students to read any of a hundred novels. The flexible scheduling concept has a broadening effect on both materials and activities in the curriculum. As the flexible schedule becomes developed with time and takes hold of the school, a different approach to curriculum construction will evolve. Team effort will have a telling influence on the curriculum. The curriculum of the flexible-scheduled school cannot be expressed in terms of specific chapters in selected books. Instead, the curriculum is organized around learning outcomes expressed in behavioral terms. The emphasis in constructing the curriculum for the teacher is on selecting processes. The materials for developing the process are often selected by the students, although the teacher is the guide in this process. For example, a behavioral outcome in social studies might be effective citizenship. To achieve this goal, several processes could be selected by the student. He could approach the topic through historical reading or by a careful study of the political structure at any level of our government. The curriculum would necessarily be functionally specific but leave the approach up to the student, with his teacher's help always at hand.

This does not mean a return to the days of "do as you want" education. It does mean that students have a choice of alternate paths to get to teacher-determined processes. Each route a student takes will be geared to his interest and ability level. However, an attempt will be made to use as many resource materials and see as many alternate choices as possible.

## The Process of Learning

In the flexible schedule the student is not expected to learn about science and literature. He is expected to do the work of science and develop a feeling for literature.

Each student becomes an investigator. He selects a problem, often with the teacher's help, and does the business of critical investigation. The thrill and advantage of discovery is not the property of an Archimedes or Einstein exclusively. It is the right of each youngster. While every student will not take a new step into the unknown of knowledge, each can have the pleasure of finding out what others have learned. He experiences the thrill of discovery on the individual level each time he discovers an idea new to him, even though the discovery might not be new to man.

Writing a poem or short story is the business of the student of English. It is, for example, more important for students than learning about the lives of authors. Once a student has done some writing of his own, he will be more apt to want to learn about the poets of the ages. The quality of a student's work is judged against his own ability, not against the rest of civilization's store of literature.

There is importance in each activity in which a student engages. The teacher helps the student learn with every discussion, every assignment, and every consideration. The flexible schedule provides opportunities for these critical learning experiences. Group teaching does not insure group learning. Individuals learn singly, not as part of a cooperative enterprise. The flexible schedule maximizes individuality in learning. It frees the student from the restraints of others.

### Old Customs and New Situations

The flexible-scheduled school is one which has multiple standards for students. This may mean an end to honor rolls, valedictorian selections, and tests, tests, and more standardized tests. Each of these practices assumes all students are running in the same race and have the same potential for finishing it. In the flexible-scheduled school the standard for each student is determined by his own capacities, bounded by his experiences, and stimulated by his interests. While there are certain basic expectations planned for all students, there are not group norms as a goal of the educators.

We cannot have individualized instruction and maintain a single standard for all students. The goals of the flexible schedule are different for each pupil. Conflicting alternative courses of action, and there are always various courses of action for any learning situation, make it imperative that we give students the skills to make critical judgments. The focus is on logical thinking and not on fact storage.

The end of education is to maximize the development of the individual, not to limit his potential by arbitrary standards. The secondary school has the obligation to give students a full image of appreciations and understanding. We cannot afford to teach functionally specific skills and delimited knowledge as if it were not on the threshold of obsolescence. Students in a flexible-scheduled school should have experiences in the fine as well as the practical arts.

### Preparing Students

Before a school inaugurates a flexible schedule, it is necessary that the students be prepared for this new experience. By the time a youngster gets to the seventh or ninth grade he usually has formed some firm notions about school, teachers, and himself in the network. The attitudes a student has about learning are not always positive. He rebels at the regimentation that has been imposed on him. He is accustomed to a teacher who talks to "boys and girls" or to "class" and not to him individually, unless there is a single answer response requested or unless something is unusual. The student is used to being considered one of the group, and it is the group to which his references are generally made.

The flexible schedule changes all of this. Before the student can accept this change in terms of behaving in a new way in school, however, he needs to be given a clear understanding of why the school is to be arranged differently. Mere understanding of the reasons, regardless of their lofty nature, for this new framework will not insure or even suggest that students will become more self-directed or more interested in their own learning. Change in learning behavior takes time and effort on the part of both teachers and students.

A good beginning is helpful in providing a smooth transition from a traditional way of working in school to the flexible-schedule way. Before a school makes the transformation, it is wise to use a variety of means to let students know what the flexible schedule will be like. Articles in the school newspaper, discussions in classes, school-wide assemblies, printed descriptive bulletins, and releases to the local newspaper are all beneficial ways to create a favorable attitude toward the new school schedule. Before going into the flexible schedule, it is advisable to spend a year in studying the concept and introducing the idea into the community. Discussions of this process can be found elsewhere.[1]

## It Takes Time

It takes time for students to become accustomed to learning in the way the flexible schedule implies. Long after everyone knows what group meets which module, there will still be difficulty in getting students as involved in the learning process as the staff will desire. It is difficult for students to act in school in this new way.

What student in a traditional class has been an active discussant in each class every time it has met? The bounds of time, the lectures of the teacher, and the restrictions placed on everyone's involvement by group size have kept the student from verbalizing ideas on a regular and complete basis. A student could get through school to a diploma by being able to use only two words, yes and no. The teacher has supplied too many of the questions for our students if they are to internalize their school content. It will take a large measure of skill on the teacher's part to stimulate real seminar discussions. Providing the time and limiting the group size will not do the job alone.

Independent study is not an activity which becomes a reality by the mere creation of the resources and the opportunity. Here again it takes the consistent and imaginative work of the teacher, plus a lot of experience or trial and error on the students' part to make the activity productive. There will be many false starts on a student's part. He will select problems that are too broad, he will have difficulty finding materials, he will put off important work until a deadline is at hand, and he will spend too little time on some activities and too much on others. All of these problems, though, are an essential part of the process of getting used to a flexible schedule. More important, these are difficulties one must overcome to be an effective thinker.

The measure of how well a program helps a student body is determined by how much the students improve as the program is operative. If a student learned to listen to teachers over six to nine years as the essential mode of instruction, it may take much longer than six to nine weeks to learn to be almost completely productive in the flexible schedule.

CHAPTER 5

# Teachers and a Professional Role

Schools employing flexible schedules submit positive reactions from staff members to this organization for learning. Principals report that teachers react favorably to their increased interaction with students which flexible scheduling allows. Principal Harold Kindy, Shawnee Junior High School, Lima, Ohio, maintains his teachers like their flexible schedule because it gives them "more influence over the learning situation." Teachers at this Ohio school can arrange the use of time to the maximum advantage of their students.

Enthusiasm is difficult to maintain every day in the regular schedule. The deadening repetition of the traditional schedule is taken out of content presentation when, instead of five presentations a day in the usual teaching assignment, the teacher gives only one or two group explanations every day in a flexible schedule. Therefore, the teacher can put energy and planning into each presentation. Teaching becomes a series of new experiences; expansion of the guidance role with students results and adds to the teacher's satisfaction.

The Mary Potter High School in Oxford, North Carolina, has a sizable proportion of students coming from several small rural schools with diverse programs. Thus, the students have had various exposures to basic content when they get to high school. The flexible schedule, Principal J. V. Morris reports, allows the teachers to regroup students according to their needs. Therefore, variations in students' preparation can be complemented by flexible scheduling. This makes it possible for teachers to fill in voids or provide enrichment experiences for students when such needs exist.

Collins T. Haan, the principal of the Fremont High School, Sunnyvale, California, reports "those teachers who have been involved in our flexible scheduling program like it. They are even enthusiastic about it." The flexible schedule, according to Mr. Haan, allows the Fremont faculty to provide for the differences in learning, interest, and ability of students in advanced high school work.

A word of caution. Teachers often express skepticism about flexible scheduling proposals the first time they hear them. The thought of changing the way they teach can be threatening. The educational leader who introduces the concept of variability in scheduling needs to be prepared to calm fears and remove anxiety feelings. After all, it is natural to be immediately and mildly defensive about challenges to what one has been doing for some time. With intensive study and a talking partnership between the principal and the teachers, anxieties and uncertainties will give way to conviction and a commitment to flexible scheduling.

As teachers become aware of the possibilities of flexible scheduling, care should be taken to underscore the potential advantages to teachers as well as to students. The benefit to students is the primary reason, of course, for considering a flexible schedule; but the positive advantage to teachers should not be ignored. This is not to advocate minimizing or skirting the potential negative factors of a flexible schedule. Problems must be identified and carefully considered. However experience has shown that the pitfalls will be easier to see than the promises of the concept.

The best way to insure acceptance of a flexible schedule, according to Dr. James L. Olivero, principal of the Poway High School, Poway, California, is "to involve the staff in every decision made related to the new design for teaching."

## It Is Not Necessarily for All

A school going into a flexible schedule does not have to schedule all students for all courses in the flexible schedule. However, it is more difficult technically to get the job done when all in the school are not on a flexible schedule, particularly when the scheduling job is being done by hand.

There are some who advocate a concept of gradualism in going into a flexible schedule. The reasoning goes like this. The idea of flexible scheduling is sound, but it should be introduced gradually to allow students and teachers to adjust to it.

First, one department or grade level will use it, then the rest of the staff can observe it for possible future use. Second, if all does not turn out well, an adjustment can be made and the school can retreat to the traditional method. Several pitfalls are built into this view. In the first place, it is difficult, if not impossible, to have some students going to study halls and others working in various stations on independent study projects. Students are confused in their operational behavior as to when they are free to use a language laboratory, for example, and when the "traditional" class is using it. When the flexible schedule students use the language laboratory, it will be on self-determined work. When the traditionally scheduled students use the laboratory, it is generally on teacher-directed activities.

The gradual approach raises the complex question also about teaching behavior. A flexible schedule requires a new approach to instruction. Teachers are hard pressed to be chameleons. One hour, they are to talk, talk, talk, to a class of thirty in a traditional class; next hour they are expected to listen, evaluate, and stimulate a group of seven in an inquiry group. Few teachers can make the transition effectively. If a school staff is convinced that flexible scheduling is good for some, why isn't it good for everyone? If it isn't good for everyone, then why should it be used for some?

What does experience show in regard to the advisability of all teachers going into flexible schedule at one time? The evidence is positive. Ridgewood High School, Norridge, Illinois; El Dorado High School, El Dorado, Arkansas; Lakeview High School, Decatur, Illinois; Brookhurst Junior High School, Anaheim, California; Holland High School, Holland, Michigan, and others have done it with success. Of course, there was no small amount of preplanning and faculty study. If the entire school is not on flexible schedule, there is an unfortunate tendency to restrict these helpful discussions to only those who are personally involved.

At the same time, as one mentions the reasons why it is wise for the whole school to implement a flexible schedule, it must be pointed out that there are other schools who have introduced the flexible schedule successfully on a piecemeal basis. Their development is slower and there is early evidence that they are having more difficulty reaching their stated goals. Individual school situations will help a staff take a position on both the extent and pace to be used in implementing their flexible schedule.

### A Summary of Advantages and Disadvantages

The advantages and disadvantages given by the educators in the thirty-three schools surveyed who have used a flexible schedule are summarized below.

| Advantages for Teachers | Disadvantages for Teachers |
|---|---|
| 1. Provides a Means for Pacing the Instruction to an Individual Student's Needs | 1. Danger of Not Giving Enough Time to One Subject |
| 2. Allows Teachers to Make Decisions about the Length and Frequency of Learning Activities | 2. Requires more Time and cooperative Effort of Teachers in Making the Schedule |
| 3. Gives Teachers Time to Work with Small Groups and Individuals | 3. Possibility of too little Identification of a Student with his Teachers |
| 4. Takes Unnecessary Repetition out of the Teacher's Day | 4. Is Difficult to Schedule |
| 5. Places Increased Responsibility on Students for Learning | 5. Requires Teachers to Change their Teaching Patterns |
| 6. Provides the Opportunity to Use Resource Experts for a large Group of Students in an Economical Way for the Resource Person | 6. Is Not Understood by the Public or even by All Teachers |

FIGURE EIGHT

One significant point which recurs in discussions of flexible scheduling with teachers who are involved is that even when they see disadvantages to the flexible schedule, they generally feel the advantages outweigh the disadvantages. The positive reactions tend to be higher among staffs which have had a part in setting up the new schedule. Maximum involvement appears to be highly correlated with positive feelings of satisfaction on the part of teachers.

Teachers with a number of years of teaching experience can find the flexible scheduling concept alarming when first described. But as the seasoned instructor becomes involved, it has been demonstrated that it is the longer tenure teachers who are the stronger advocates of flexible scheduling. A report from the Evanston High School staff in Evanston, Illinois, confirmed this.

Teachers in their first year or two of teaching tend to see more value or at least they tend to express more interest in the large-group instruction a flexible schedule allows. To beginning teachers the instructional process is apparently centered around the exposition of content by instructors. The experienced teacher usually puts more value in student interaction and involvement than the fledgling instructor.

### Acceptance of Flexible Scheduling

The degree to which teachers in schools using flexible schedules react positively appears to be in direct proportion to the amount of attention the administrator gives to it. Principals, who are educational leaders, who talk about instructional techniques with their staff and who give approval in positive terms to flexible scheduling practices, have a definite influence on the teaching staff's acceptance of flexible scheduling. Administrative approval goes a long way toward getting a practice favorably received in a school.

In the seventeen of the thirty-three schools surveyed that were trying flexible schedules on a limited basis, it was noted that the teachers who reported reservations about the concept also reported the principals had a "wait and see" attitude about the concept. In one of these schools a teacher reports:

> Our principal introduced the idea of flexible scheduling to us and gave us a lot of descriptive materials from the journals. When two other teachers and I formulated a plan, he said we could try it. At the same time, he made it very clear he was skeptical that flexible

scheduling had any value for us. We are trying it now. Up to now he has not commented on our progress. (The implementation was in its eighth month at the time of the survey.) It would be helpful to us to know what he feels about our efforts.

The teachers in this school need the support the administrator can give. Without his interest the program will have less chance of permanent acceptance.

Flexible scheduling is a way to get more efficiency into a teacher's day. At the same time, it introduces new challenges and pressures which are not a part of the isolated classroom teaching situation. The flexible schedule requires more professional communication and co-operative planning. Those who do not like to work with their fellow teachers have difficulty in a flexible scheduling plan. Of course the question is: will cooperative planning and teaching benefit students? If the answer is affirmative, then steps need to be taken to encourage this new professional activity.

The self-contained classroom puts a teacher in the position of being the absolute authority in knowledge about content and methodology. The flexible schedule tends to break down monolithic teaching; teachers become dependent upon each other. While the new associations are professionally and personally beneficial, they are not always easy for all to accept. Here again the school administrator must exercise his leadership in cultivating a secure and rewarding atmosphere.

Students respond positively to the flexible schedule if the instructor is geared to their interests and growth. Negative student reactions to flexible scheduling practices can be traced to what goes on within the schedule and not to the schedule itself. There is good reason to believe students react in an equally negative fashion to poor instructional practices in the self-contained classroom.

### An Expression of Confidence in Teachers

Flexible scheduling practices are manifestations of supreme faith in teachers. Each teacher who participates in the construction of the school schedule is exercising professional judgments and making important technical decisions. The determination of the length and frequency of a class meeting is a professional judgment. Decisions about the size of learning groups, the number of small and large groups, and so forth are based on the kind of instruction the teacher expects to employ. The traditional class schedule does not allow teachers to make decisions about these matters, but the flexible schedule puts into teachers' hands control over these potentially important variables in the instructional process. By expecting teachers to make such judgments, confidence is expressed in their professional competency.

The formula established for learning groups varies according to the content, the instructional procedures to be employed, and the significance of the activity or subject. Content which requires a generous amount of explanation will imply more large-group meetings than content which can best be mastered by independent student effort. If the instructional aim of the study of a particular subject is to develop appreciations or formulate attitudes, there will be more small discussion groups than large-group presentations. Attitudes and convictions are evolved, according to the theory which undergirds flexible scheduling, by interaction with others, by trying out views in discussions, and by listening to others translate their impressions of a concept.

Process mastery is the result of repetition and action. Therefore teachers must design problem situations or propose exercises which call for repetitive tasks which are sequentially ordered. Once the sequence of problem solving is reenforced, understanding will result.

As teachers call for fewer small-group meetings, they are putting the burden for learning on the individual. Independent study takes on increased importance. The formula can vary within a course as well as between courses. That is, a teacher or teachers may require more large-group presentations in the early stages of instruction and decrease the presentation sessions later in favor of added time for either small-group discussion or independent study. The form of organization selected for each course should be related to the requirements needed for mastery. The schedule set in September is not absolute. It can be altered or left intact for weekly, monthly, or six weeks' periods. This will be discussed at length elsewhere.

Teachers who know their students and have established clearly defined instructional goals are in the best position to set up learning-group specifications. To insist that goals be twisted and learning activities be compressed or strung out to meet rigid time requirements is a travesty on the wisdom of teachers and a hindrance to a school's doing the very best for every student.

Asking teachers to make decisions about these matters is a new experience for both teachers and administrators. Determination of learning-group specifications is, however, one of the more important functions of every teacher. As educators develop increased understanding of the teacher-learning process, more emphasis will be put on the construction of course learning groups.

## The Claim for More, More

Some critics of flexible scheduling claim that teachers will not make independent judgments about the number of learning groups for a course. They say that if the music teacher requests five class meetings a week, for example, the homemaking teacher will want at least five. Others say the status of a subject is set by number of class sessions.

Experience has shown that this is not the case. Teachers can make critical judgments about the time requirements of their subjects and can request varying numbers of large and small groups for different courses. In schools where teachers were unrealistic about the number of class sessions they required, there was evidence that the staff was not clear on their course goals and vague on their conviction about the kinds of learning experiences needed to master the content. Also, the rationale of the flexible schedule has not been accepted, if indeed it is understood, when teachers make up specifications based on criteria other than what is appropriate for understanding ideas or developing skills.

If a course has its only value set by the number of meetings it requires, it has little real worth. Students are quick to spot a diluted soup in the cafeteria or diluted instruction in the classroom. Subjects which can be learned in fewer meetings than five a week will be selected by students if they see an advantage in them. As a matter of fact, Ridgewood High in Norridge, Illinois, reports that their courses which meet for fewer than five days a week are among the most popular in the school.

Because a teacher is not meeting with a formal group every day does not mean students are not working on the subject each day. Instruction in a class can be given in typing only two or three times a week, but students will be using a typewriter to practice and to do their work every day. Likewise, a student can master some science, history, and industrial arts courses without daily meetings.

## Grades—A Problem for Teachers

How often we hear about the problems teachers have in determining student grades! Both teachers and students are quick to point this out as a problem which bothers them in a traditional schedule. How, then, will it be affected by a flexible schedule? Grading in a flexible schedule should be easier because the small-group teachers should know more about their students' knowledge and understandings.

The small-group teacher is the logical one to assign the grade. He knows the student and sees him use ideas. The testing which goes on in large groups may play a part in the grade, but the best judge is the teacher who listens and sees the student as he works at his level of ability.

A letter or numerical grade is of little worth anyway. We have probably paid too much attention to grading procedures to the detriment of teaching practices. Grades serve essentially as a device for communicating with parents about Johnny's progress. Those who use grades as a club are weak teachers. Teaching strength is made visible by the motivation students have to do work in the subject. When students work on projects within a subject on their interest and ability level, the grade-crutch is not needed by even the staunchest advocates of the red pencil.

Grades have always been a problem. They will continue to be a problem, hopefully not as big a problem, with a flexible schedule. The flexible schedule's small-group class provides youngsters with a better way of getting teacher and group approval, through quality of performance. The work youngsters do in independent study gives them an opportunity to accomplish their own instructional goals. There is more satisfaction for many from a sophisticated science project than from an A on a paper. The A is easily determined when the quality science study is completed. As teachers become involved in working on class preparation and as they come to know students in an intimate way, the concern for the normal curve of distribution is eliminated.

## *It Is Largely the Same*

The process of discovery is much the same whether it is in a college researcher's laboratory or in a class of slow learners. The difference is in depth of perception and profundity of thought. Differences are in degree not in kind. As a poem was written by Dylan Thomas, he had the same order of thought arrangement as the high school student does when he writes his poem.

Teaching in high school is a process of stimulating sensitivity and understanding. The effective teachers are the ones who bring the best out in every student. What is good work for Henry may be a poor production for Jane. On the other hand, it may be Henry who gained the greater advantage if he went as far as he could in knowing and appreciating and if Jane did not reach her comparative limits.

Flexible scheduling, in the final analysis, is a manifestation that a school which employs it is process oriented. That is, this school is interested in students learning how to learn. The content, whatever it is, is the means whereby youngsters learn to sort facts and to develop fundamental skills. All content is a means whereby youngsters learn to discriminate, appreciate, relate, and create.

As teachers look at flexible scheduling, they must grapple with the issue of why a student comes to school each day. Is he to learn science which will be outdated a year or decade from now? Is the purpose to study literature different in form and style from what is to be the mode of his adult years? Are the issues considered in the social studies class the ones that will plague society in the future?

If one holds the view that culture is a growing, expanding accumulation of man's development, then we cannot afford to be satisfied with anything less than teaching youngsters how to think and how to act. The study of affairs and beliefs of the past is done as a guide to the future, but not as the final guide. A better aim of instruction is the one which uses classroom content as a basis of knowing how to know more.

Teaching processes of thinking, evaluating, discovering, and creating are the ageless important business of education. The Civil War or the Sit-Ins in southern cities are largely the same, only means to a more important end. If they are contributing forces, teachers really do not teach subject matter as much as they teach processes. Flexible scheduling provides for teachers to guide students in process acquisition; then it gives learners time to get the job done.

## Team Teaching

IndiFlexS calls for teaching teams. Wherever more than one teacher is required to instruct the number of students in a course, a team is established. The small and large group with independent study pattern can be used without team teaching, but the advantages of team teaching to both students and teachers makes its use judicious.

Teams of teachers can be organized in a variety of ways. There is merit of different kinds for each of the arrangements. IndiFlexS organizes teams by subject matter and by course. That is, all teachers of one subject area who teach the same course are members of a team. An alternate method of organizing teams is by blocks of students. In this method teachers of several disciplines who have a common group of students are on a team. This is the method used by The University of Chicago Laboratory School Model. The IndiFlexS option of organizing the teams around subject disciplines is preferred because of the success this organization has had and because of the ease with which a school can move eventually to a nongraded curriculum.

If a team of teachers is responsible for the instruction of all students who take a particular course, the team makes cooperative decisions about content, assignments, and both student and content evaluation. However, one teacher is responsible for giving the lectures and for the broad evaluation of the total group of students. The teacher responsible for the assembly group presentation serves as chairman of the team. As such he is responsible for calling meetings of the team, communicating with department heads and carrying out the administrative chores of ordering materials, submitting scheduling recommendations, and so forth. The chairman of the team is an equal partner with the other team members.[1]

Working closely with the team's chairman, the team members who work with the inquiry groups have a demanding job. They must remain supple, work on the spot, and consult individually and frequently with students. The inquiry-group teachers provide informative feedback to the teacher of the assembly groups as to the students' reactions to the presentations.

In large schools some teachers of the assembly groups may not meet with inquiry groups. This will not be likely in smaller schools, and it may not ever be advisable. If an assembly-group teacher's schedule permits, it is wise for him to have at least one inquiry group. This helps the assembly-group teacher keep in touch with what goes on in the inquiry group. In a school of six hundred or more students it probably will not be necessary for any teachers to serve on more than two teams. Teachers' interest and time is too fragmented if they find it necessary to work in too many areas.

The teacher who is best at working with the inquiry groups should be assigned to these groups; the member of the team who does the finest job of making assembly-group presentations should have this assignment. It is significant to point out that teachers usually will select the kind of assignment they can do most effectively once they understand each role. Neither teaching task—the assembly-group teaching or the inquiry-group teaching—is more important than the other.

The teacher of the inquiry group will find it more difficult to develop the skills necessary to work in these groups than in the assembly groups. Lecturing is a customary part of the teaching process. But listening to students to detect their perceptions, stimulating student discussion without monopolizing it, making suggestions for resources, and connecting old ideas to new ones are teaching functions that require particular skills which teachers have not had to develop. It is in the inquiry groups that real internalization of ideas takes place and enduring values and attitudes are grounded. Thus, teachers with successes in inquiry groups report this is a most rewarding teaching role to fill, according to our survey.

As the schedule is constructed, the determination of who will work with each group must be made. While the administrator has to make the final assignment, he will be ratifying personal choices if the staff are allowed to make their preferences known. Six of the thirty-three administrators in our survey stated that teachers selected the role the principal would select for them to fill, and no other respondents reported the contrary. However, this was not a question included in our inquiry.

As with varying class-size organization, team teaching should not be inaugurated without considerable and detailed staff study, discussion, and agreement. An extensive and intensive faculty study which includes all the staff must be carried on over a period of time, perhaps a year. This will allow full investigation and frank expression of opinion.

## *The Teacher's Schedule*

Like the student's schedule, it is impossible to picture one schedule for a teacher and have it be valid for all other staff members. Each teacher's schedule is built around the instructional services he performs. The teacher who makes assembly-group presentations, for example, will need more preparation time than a teacher who may work almost exclusively with inquiry groups. Those teachers who are a part of a teaching team will require time for teams to meet during the school week. Department heads will need time in the week to meet with the principal and other department heads to coordinate the program and to handle routine administrative matters. All of these activities are too important to relegate to after hours' chance considerations. Of primary importance in structuring any school day is to provide time for teachers to study, to read, to correct students' work, and to evaluate individual and group progress. All of these time-consuming vital parts of teaching need to be taken into consideration as the schedule is constructed.

In Figure Nine the formula used in IndiFlexS for distributing a teacher's school day is given. This must be modified to suit particular conditions in various situations, but it is generally in harmony with an economical and sound use of teachers' time. The variable around which the most adjustment will be made in various situations concerns the department head. In schools where the department heads have class-visitation responsibilities, more time will need to be given for this function. Since there seems to be a trend away from this practice in schools of sufficient size to employ an assistant principal for curriculum or a curriculum coordinator, time for supervision was not included.

| Time Per Week | | Professional Activity | Distribution | For Whom |
| Hours | Modules | | | |
|---|---|---|---|---|
| 5 | 10 | Class Preparation | Equal each Day | All Teachers |
| 1 | 2 | Team Conferences | At Least Two each Week | Team Members |
| ½ | 1 | Team Leader | Varies | Team Leader |
| 1* | 2* | Assembly Group Presenter | Varies | Only Presenter |
| 5 | 10 | Department Heads | Varies | Department Heads Only |
| 2** | 4** | Work with Special Students on Independent Study | Varies | Any Teacher |
| As Assigned | As Assigned | Assembly Groups | By Set Sequence | Any Teacher |
| As Assigned | As Assigned | Inquiry Groups | By Set Sequence | Any Teacher |
| As Assigned | As Assigned | Instructional Materials Center Assistance | Varies | Any Teacher |
| 1 | 2 | Department Meeting | Varies | All Members |

FIGURE NINE

*For each assembly group presentation a teacher gives, two modules
  of preparation are provided.
**Students during particular advanced or remedial studies must meet
  with teachers on a regular basis. Time is allowed in the schedule for
  preparation for these activities.

The use of IndiFlexS puts heavy requirements on the use of the
library or, hopefully, an instructional materials center. This is the
heart of the school. Much of the success of the independent study activities will depend on both the services students can get and the
availability of resources in the instructional materials center. While
this is discussed in some detail in Chapter 6, it is appropriate here to
emphasize its importance. It is recommended that teachers, in addition to the usual library and audiovisual staff, be scheduled in the
instructional materials center to assist students on their individual
learning projects. Where possible, teachers' offices should be located

near the instructional materials center so there is easy access for students to teachers. The number and content area speciality of teachers assigned to the instructional materials center each period or module will vary from school to school. The larger schools, of at least fifteen hundred students, will likely want to have an English teacher, a mathematics teacher, and a social studies teacher assigned there each module of the day. Science teachers will likely be available in or near the science laboratories for consultation with students each module of the day. These assignments are a part of the day's teaching service and should be taken into consideration when the schedule is constructed.

IndiFlexS does not require a larger number of teachers than a good traditional schedule. Where then, one might ask, does the time come from to provide increased preparation, time for team and department meetings, and added preparation time for assembly-group teachers? Of course, the time comes from the economies effected by the assembly groups and by the independent study time. It is more economical of student and teacher time to give one large or assembly-group presentation than it is to give instruction in four or five smaller groups. There is a saving of teacher time in the independent study time for students as well. However, the small or inquiry groups will place a drain on staff time since it takes two or three times as many teacher hours to handle two or three inquiry groups than a traditional class. Usually these will not meet on a daily basis. This means that there is time for these new professional activities to be scheduled during the week.

Some students may wish to work on subjects outside of formal classes. The staff may feel that particular benefit can be given to youngsters with severe learning problems or with high ability. In these cases some of the staff can be assigned to these pupils for individual work. This should be a part of the teachers' formal responsibility and worked into the schedule.

A school schedule which does not provide time for teachers to plan adequately for their classes, to meet with students for individual help, and to confer with other teachers is not being fair to the students or wise in its use of potential teaching talent. IndiFlexS puts a high value on both individual and group preparation and evaluation by teachers.

CHAPTER 6

# Facilities and Equipment for Flexible Scheduling

As the schedule a school uses changes, there will also be modifications in the use of space in a school building. Often principals contend they cannot use one scheduling innovation or another because of inadequate facilities. This is more often an excuse than a reason. IndiFlexS can be used in nearly any school. While it is true that some adjustments will need to be made in the way facilities are used, and while perhaps even minor structural alterations may be called for, there are few school plants which are so out of date or in such disrepair that IndiFlexS cannot be implemented, perhaps with some abridgments.

Of course, facilities do stand as a force to be reckoned with as a schedule is constructed. As pointed out, the facilities available are variables which need priority consideration as the flexible schedule is considered.

Educational Facilities Laboratories, Inc., a Ford Foundation subsidized agency, has supported projects and helped devise new arrangements of school space. E.F.L. has prepared a series of booklets which give floor plans and pictures of schools constructed for a flexible schedule.[1]

79

## Redistribution Rather Than More Space

IndiFlexS does not necessitate remodeling or adding to a school facilitiy; however, it does require a redistribution of facilities and equipment. First, there must be a place for assembly groups to meet. Accommodations used for this kind of instruction vary from specially designed lecture rooms with acoustical treatment, special speaking and audiovisual systems, and modern student furniture to rooms formerly used for large study halls, cafeterias, or auditoriums. Superior instruction can go on in an old, archaic school building just as well as it can in a sleek, new structure of the latest design and space distribution. From the survey which is a part of this report it is interesting to note that some of the most flexible school schedules came from schools built prior to 1950. New buildings are not requirements for the use of new teaching procedures. Admittedly, the facilities and equipment of a school contribute to what both teachers and students can do in the school. There is good reason to assert with positive certainty that flexible scheduling practices, as advocated in IndiFlexS, can be employed in varying degrees in any school that can accommodate a traditional school schedule.

## Not Less Either

A few theorists have projected the notion that the flexible schedule will save the amount of space needed in school construction. This contention is rejected on the basis of the experience of schools which have used the flexible schedule for several years. The experience seems clear that as the flexible schedule follows its logical consequence and provokes increased independent study, more specialized spaces are called for. Space usage is both redistributed and saturated in the traditional school plant. Traditional classrooms become learning laboratories, the library becomes an instructional materials center, and the shop spaces are used as a place for independent study.

## Facilities Developed After the Program

It is recommended that the staff concentrate on the development of the instructional program before launching into widespread remodeling or building additions to complement a new program. Too often the buildings a school district enjoys are strides ahead of the use the staff sees for them. For example, it was folly for one Kentucky school administration to knock out walls, put in movable curtains, and add a number of individual study carrels when the faculty still taught in their isolated classes of five periods for five days. The facility changes were annoying to a staff which neither understood nor wanted them.

Louis Sullivan, the noted architect, was reputed to have enunciated the "form follows function" doctrine. This concept seems valuable for considering facilities in the flexible schedule. The program should come first; the facilitiy modifications should follow. School patrons are more likely to give enthusiastic approval to new building or re-modeling programs when a successful program requiring building re-finements, additions, or changes is in operation than when such a program exists only in the vision of the chief school administrator.

## The Heart of the School

The heart of the IndiFlexS school is the instructional materials center. The instructional materials center, hereafter frequently referred to as the IMC, is more than a combination library and audiovisual reposi-tory of materials. The IMC is a place for both student and teacher study activity. It combines the elements of the traditional library— books, materials, and professional librarian's service—with those of a laboratory with individual work spaces and areas for group and in-dividual activity. The IMC usually has a quiet zone where individual study can be pursued without interruption and a noise zone where students can type, listen to electronc tapes and recordings with ear-phones, and work with adding machines, calculators, duplicating, and other office machines.

The IMC is staffed with a librarian and secretarial assistants. As the school uses IndiFlexS over a period of years, there will likely be more staff additions needed in the IMC than in other departments within the school. There are a number of arrangements of space which are appropriate for the construction of the material center. While outside of the province of this discussion to detail these, it may be helpful here to state a preference for a single, unified materials center. Some schools have built smaller centers near each cluster of classrooms in a department. There are both potential control and efficiency problems from this arrangement. When the school's collection of books, transparencies, and other resource materials are dispersed, they cannot be used with the ease possible when one large IMC is established.

Figure Ten gives a layout of the instructional materials center used effectively at Washington Township's North Central High School in Indianapolis, Indiana. This center provides space for students to work individually and in groups. Rooms are set up for programmed learning use, for materials preparation, and for faculty study.

INSTRUCTIONAL MATERIALS CENTER AT NORTH CENTRAL HIGH SCHOOL, INDIANAPOLIS, INDIANA

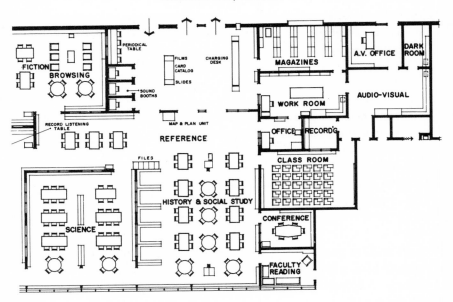

FIGURE TEN

School buildings which have been in use for a number of years will be able to expand their library to a real materials center with the use of IndiFlexS. Because IndiFlexS needs fewer traditional classrooms, since a substantial block of students' time is allocated to independent study and inquiry group classes, there is sufficient space for an instructional materials center. Inquiry classes require half as much space as traditional classes.

The instructional materials center contains books, magazines, pamphlets, pictures, maps, museum pieces, mock-ups, films, filmstrips, recordings, electronic tapes, slides, and all the learning aids and reference materials the school owns. Those items not housed in the IMC are noted in the reference card catalog with their home location specified. This gives the teacher or student the knowledge of their existence and location in the school for possible use.

The significant characteristic of the IMC is the activity it engenders. Students should be free to use the IMC for as much time and in as many ways as possible. The emphasis of the professional staff is on service. They will be required to work continually with students in locating, ordering, and selecting particular resources for a student's individual project or for an inquiry group study.

As the percentage of time students spend in independent study increases, the space of the IMC must expand correspondingly. There must be room in the IMC to seat at least thirty per cent of the student body at one time for a senior high school. Of course, less space will be needed for a junior high school IndiFlexS program.

The quiet zone in the IMC will have a few large tables. Most of the students will be able to use individual study carrels. In other sections of the IMC special rooms or areas will be provided for functionally specific tasks. Viewing rooms, listening equipment, typing rooms, and so forth require special facilities in the IMC.

## Inquiry-Group Rooms

Since inquiry-group rooms do not need the space of traditional classrooms, these can be divided by vision screens, even of a homemade variety, or by bookcases in an established building. The inquiry-group rooms should have the furniture arranged so that the participants in the class can see each other, face to face. This arrangement will stimulate communication and allow the participants to establish an intimacy helpful for stimulating discussion. A large group of sectional tables is recommended for use in the inquiry classrooms, although the traditional school furniture will be usable.

The inquiry-group classroom needs no more room than for seven to fifteen students. Some principals have found it advantageous to divide some rooms into smaller sections, perhaps to accommodate three inquiry groups, while other rooms will be able to house only two of the larger size groups, probably for fifteen students each. Several discussions can go on at one time in a room if the groups are isolated by vision screens. Once a discussion begins, the participants will block out the sounds beyond their particular group.

Many, if not most, schools will find it unnecessary to have more than one inquiry group in a room. This is determined by the space availability of the school. Extra space in the traditionally sized room can be used for project activity of students or perhaps for teachers' offices.

## The Assembly-Group Room

The assembly-group room needs to be large enough to accommodate the largest assembly-group class. As has been noted, the established school sometimes can use a cafeteria, an auditorium, or an old study hall. The assembly-group room should be equipped with a simultaneous voice amplifying and recording system. This will make it possible for the teacher to be heard as he speaks in a normal, conversational tone. At the same time, the presentation can be recorded for storage and use in the instructional materials center. Students who missed a presentation or want to review it can listen to the tape of the class in the IMC. Schools which record the assembly-group presentations sometimes find it helpful for the teachers who make the presentations to listen to their lectures. This can be a valuable tool for self-evaluation and improvement, the teachers who have used it report.

The assembly room should also be equipped with an overhead projector. This replaces the chalk board and does an infinitely better job of projecting visuals. During the planning time the teacher who gives the assembly presentation can prepare dynamic transparencies which allow the teacher to show as well as tell when ideas are being presented. The noncertified aide can be helpful to the teacher in the mechanical production of these transparencies. Once used, the transparency goes to the IMC for cataloging and use by students and other teachers.

The location of the teacher in the assembly-group room should be such that he is at a forty-five degree angle from all students in the room. This gives the teacher visual control and the students an easy sight-line to the teacher. The arrangement of the room should also be such that students can take notes and tests without the interference of others.

While it is impossible to give an adequate formula for the number of assembly-group rooms needed until after the staff has made decisions about the extent of use of the assembly classes, it may be helpful to report the experience of three schools that have approached the IndiFlexS model. The first school was a three-year high school of nine hundred pupils. They had two assembly rooms with a capacity of three hundred in one room and eighty in another. The second school was a six-year junior-senior high school of one thousand forty students. This school had two large-group rooms, one to take care of two hundred and twenty and the other for ninety students. The third school was a three-year junior high school of six hundred and twenty students. This school had three assembly-group rooms: one for seventy, another for one hundred and fifty, and the third for two hundred students. In none of these schools was the faculty's program such that the assembly group rooms were utilized all the modules of the day. With a fifteen-module day and with five different daily schedules, there is the potential of seventy-five assembly classes a week for each available room. Few IndiFlexS programs in schools of fifteen hundred pupils or less will call for more than two assembly rooms.

Some of the assembly groups may have as few as thirty students in them, particularly in the senior high school where enrollment in some advanced courses is limited to that number. The size of the assembly group is set by the total number of students who will profit from instruction in a large group. In other courses, the usual required ones and general appreciation courses, the assembly groups will be much larger. Some of these classes may have up to three hundred pupils, as was pointed out in Chapter 1. Decisions about space use must come after the instructional program is established.

## Teachers' Offices

When teachers are given time to do planning and to meet with students, they must be provided with an adequate place to utilize the time well. It makes more economic sense to give teachers small offices than to install them in a classroom all day. The classroom space is too large and precious to stand idle from students during teacher-preparation periods. Each teacher should have an office where he can do his course preparation and evaluation work. Also, teachers need an appropriate place to meet with students for individual conferences.

Some schools have housed several teachers in one office. Usually the offices are shared by the members of one teaching team. Vision screens are often put between the teachers' areas so that there can be simultaneous conferences with students free from distracting office activity of others.

It is difficult for the observer of the traditional school to visualize the number of conferences students and teachers will have with IndiFlexS. Individualized instruction calls for frequent consultations with teachers, both during and after school. The students need to know where the teacher can be found and, at the same time, have a place for depth discussions.

When possible the teachers' offices should surround the instructional materials center. This arrangement provides comfortable access of students to teachers and it allows the teacher convenient use of the resources in the IMC. IndiFlexS will put new requirements on teachers to be familiar with the school's instructional materials when the single text is abandoned and many students embark on customized learning activities.

### Work Spaces

Specialized work spaces need to be made for the faculty and students to carry out some of the activities IndiFlexS may inspire. For example, a photographic darkroom will be needed as visuals become more a part of the teaching-learning process. A room for duplicating special materials will be required. All of the materials for the preparation of overhead transparencies must be easily available to those who will use them.

The noncertified staff will need adequate space in which to do their important work. A single area for all of the noncertified aides is recommended. The pool of noncertified workers can operate as a team, each doing the tasks he can do best.

The addition of these work spaces, like the assembly-group rooms, does not represent an addition of space requirements to most schools.

But it does call for a redistribution of classroom space in the traditionally scheduled school.

Student project work spaces will need to be established. In addition to the carrels, conference rooms, film viewing rooms, and typing spaces in the instructional materials centers, there will need to be areas set up in art, homemaking, industrial arts, science, and physical education for independent study. These specialized laboratories will allow students to work on their own projects and at their own time. These areas should be appropriate for the kind of activities students will want to do in each area. Although these areas are an important part of the total facility use, they usually are not developed in the early stages of the use of IndiFlexS. While it is wise to dedicate the space in each area for the use of independent study, it is judicious to encourage the staff to outfit them as the program develops. Experience has shown that both art and science areas are the first and apparently easiest to develop.

Some special rooms, like typing and science laboratories, can be enlarged by merely removing a wall between two rooms. It is educationally sound and economically prudent to give typing and certain kinds of science laboratory instruction in larger classes than are usually found in a traditionally scheduled school. Substantial experience has established that students can learn to type and perform certain laboratory experiments and exercises in large groups of forty to sixty as profitably as in groups of twenty-five or so. The size of these groups is only limited, within reason, by the number of typewriters, science outfits, or necessary equipment. The major determinant in effective learning in these particular courses is the degree to which the student is involved in the learning activity. Quality instruction will not result in successful accomplishment in these activities wthout a student's effort, practice, and application. One teacher can serve many more than thirty students for some of the learning activities in these situations. Inquiry groups may be needed to supplement the laboratory work. It is folly to station one teacher in a room of a few students who are busy with skill development activities when more students could be accommodated as effectively. Few observers of a typing or laboratory class in a traditionally scheduled school will doubt this contention. The teachers like the larger classes as it frees them for more work with smaller groups and with individual students. Facilities should be modified to meet the best organization for instruction which is devised by the school's faculty.

## Technological Aids

The advance in the use of technological aids in the American public school has been slow. Yet the interest of educators in using mechanical aids wherever possible has increased over the last few years. In the future there surely will be even more interest in technological aids to instruction. Teaching machines, language laboratories, instructional television, electronic tape recordings, data processing, reading pacers, and projectional devices are some of the more promising aids for teachers to use in improving educational opportunities for students.

IndiFlexS does not prescribe the use of any of these aids, but their use can be included either on a regularly scheduled or a nonscheduled basis. Where a particular technological aid is to be used, it is put in the schedule specifications like an assembly group. This will be discussed in Chapter 8.

Some technological aids will be used on a regular basis for all students in a course. For instance, shorthand or language students may be assigned to weekly sessions in the language laboratory. The assignments for students in these courses will be supportive to the regular inquiry classes. The electronic language laboratory can give students drill experiences that will be helpful and, at the same time, save valuable class time for more important matters.

Some schools have used recordings effectively in social studies classes for supplementary source materials. Students are assigned listening exercises and go to the IMC to listen to famous speeches or reports of significant events on their own. Interesting inquiry class discussions follow as an analysis is made of these primary resources. A well-stocked recording collection can be of positive value for students as they study music appreciation or theory courses and as they investigate particular civilizations or periods in history.

The use of technological aids in the schools can be increased for students when blocks of independent study time are provided. For example, during these periods a student can work through a learning program on a teaching machine. The progress a student makes is dependent on his own effort and rate of learning. It is free of the speed or consideration of a group of students. IndiFlexS makes it possible to include the use of these teaching aids in the schedule of each student on an individual basis. In a traditional schedule when is a student free to work on programmed learning, view appropriate films, listen to helpful recordings, or use a language laboratory for drill as individually needed? The consideration of the regular use of multiple technological teaching aids is a part of the staff's investigation as the specifications for IndiFlexS are drawn up each year.

## The Scheduling Task

The school's total facilities must be considered as the schedule is constructed. It is helpful to the teachers if the principal will work out an availability list of facilities. This list should include information on the specific purpose of various rooms and set forth any limitations in use that may need to be put on them. For instance, if a certain room is to be deployed for use in one department area for particular independent study activities, this should be announced as soon as possible. The total number of potential assembly groups each week should be known before the flexible schedule considerations begin. Other particular restrictions on facilities should be brought to the faculty's attention as they begin the scheduling considerations.

CHAPTER 7

# Perspectives of Research and Evaluation

EDUCATORS WHO ARE EXPOSED to flexible scheduling for the first time often ask if research studies have concluded that it is better than a traditional schedule. The answer, of course, is no. Research has not judged a flexible schedule better than a traditional schedule.[1] Similarly no research study has or can answer the question of whether a fifty-minute period is better than a forty-minute period. The schedule a school uses is only one factor—only one variable—in any significant evaluation of a school program. What happens within the schedule is a major determinant of the quality of the school's instruction. Theoretically, the flexible organization allows teachers to do an even better job, but its existence alone does not insure better instruction or learning on the operational level. To study only a schedule, of whatever type, without a penetrating analysis of the other aspects of the school's program is to make an incomplete analysis of the school.

Comparisons can be made in the quantitative level between schedules. Factors such as class sizes, minutes per day or week of instruction, pupil-teacher ratios, and the like are helpful in getting an understanding of the school's program. In themselves they prove little. More important considerations are related to how well students accept responsibility for their own learning and how much of the teacher's talent is brought to bear on instructional problems. The school's schedule povides the vehicle for instruction, but the energy to give it power must come from the students and teachers.

At this point in the history of research in education there are not the tools, the time, or even the energy to work out a research design to compare two school schedules. The variables are too numerous (students, content, previous learning) and too complex (quality measures of discussion, independence, and so forth) to assess. Valid research needs to be able to control the variables in the design to an extent that is impracticable and impossible in a live school situation. Research has said nothing about school organizational effectiveness per se. One should not look to it for answers it is not able to give. There is a rich body of research which can aid the educator as he frames the school's schedule. Retention studies, learning theory, and teaching behavior are all fertile fields for review as decisions are made as to which organization for learning a school will adopt.

Research studies do not have to be comparative to have value for charting future action. It makes more sense to concentrate on research describing what happens to individuals and to a school as one schedule or another is employed. New means are related to new ends. There is danger in comparing one schedule with one set of goals to another schedule with a different set of goals. One difference between IndiFlexS and the traditional schedule is the emphasis IndiFlexS puts on the student's responsibility for his own learning. Another goal of IndiFlexS is to free some students from the narrow path group teaching often establishes. These, and the other IndiFlexS goals, are not given priority in the traditional schedule.

The absence of comparative research data that one given length of time for a course is significantly better than another arrangement of students' time is reason enough for educators to consider the employment of a flexible schedule. Empirical evidence is very strong that flexible schedules are helpful to students in learning and to teachers in teaching. None of the schools surveyed for this study indicated students learned any less subject matter than the reporters felt they would with a traditional schedule. Some even thought the students learned more.

It must be remembered that research in education is undergoing a reform itself. New attention is being given to imaginative, creative ideas. Instead of reducing multidimensional problems to unnatural simplicity, researchers are focusing attention on parts of projects, such as flexible scheduling, with real profit to their mission of critical inquiry and to clear understanding of the important problems involved in learning. Other researchers have wisely chosen to look at broad areas rather than microscopic parts of the whole.

## Evaluations Are Positive

Evaluation is an extremely important aspect of any educational program, and yet this often is done poorly. "It has been said that an administrator is shirking his responsibility if he does not evaluate systematically and fully the school for which he is responsible, and if he does not direct his staff in making such appraisals of the program."[2] It is true that flexible scheduling must be continuously evaluated. Evaluations by principals and teachers who have used flexible schedules have yielded empirical data which cries for the increased use of flexible schedules. One needs only to spend some time with an administrator or teacher in a school using a flexible schedule to have this verified.

The survey of the thirty-three schools using some form of flexible schedule has given a positive reaction to the flexible scheduling concept. The schools in this survey were of various sizes, from different parts of the country, and with diverse faculty backgrounds. All agreed, however, that their adaptation of the flexible scheduling concept was beneficial to their students and satisfying to their teachers. What more evidence is needed for anyone to make a searching appraisal of flexible scheduling?

The overriding point is: educators who have used flexible schedules like them, even prefer them to traditional schedules. Students in these schools do as well in terms of content mastery, the knowledgeable practitioners report, as those in a traditional schedule, if not better. In addition, the schools using flexible schedules go on to report that their teachers feel that students have a greater opportunity for (1) increasing their responsibility for learning, (2) working nearer their level ability, high and low, than in a traditional schedule, and (3) expanding the horizons of their scholastic pursuits than they had in the traditional curriculum.

## New Objectives with a New Schedule

The instructional methods of a school using a flexible schedule generally are not the same in emphasis as those in the school using a traditional schedule. For instance, in the flexible scheduled school one professional procedure is to bring the talents of several teachers on a teaching team to bear on a common instructional problem or course for a given group of students. In a traditionally scheduled school this is not the case, the school's procedure is to bring one teacher's skill and knowledge in one area to a comparatively limited group of students. The advantages of several teachers' talents are not regularly available for students in a traditionally scheduled school on a common instructional problem. Of course, students get the benefits of individual contact with many teachers in a traditionally scheduled school; but the advantage in the flexible schedule comes from the combined thinking of several teachers on one problem or one body of content.

In addition, in the flexible-scheduled school one primary objective is to place responsibility on the student for his learning. The traditionally scheduled school gives far less attention to this objective. From these few examples, it can be seen that comparisons are difficult, even impossible, because of varying program objectives. It is a fallacy to compare apples and monkeys or flexible and traditional schedules.

In terms of learning products—skill acquisition and knowledge—it has been established empirically that students learn as much as they would in the lockstep day.[3] It is hoped that a school is interested in more than skill development and fact acquisition for its students. The school's job is to teach youngsters the process by which they can solve problems, inquire, create, and improve their ability to sort ideas and establish values. The flexible schedule encourages a broad approach to learning and places emphasis on increased student involvement at his own level of competency.

The flexible-scheduled school puts stock in inquiry or small-group instruction. In the small group students interact with other students and internalize knowledge and concepts. What traditionally scheduled school can, as a practical matter, give youngsters a chance to do this to the extent they can in the flexible schedule? What research design could a local school carry out to measure these differences? Yet the testimony of practitioners gives telling evidence of the increased participation in intellectual discussion in the flexible-scheduled school.

Evaluation, the process of weighing evidence and making value judgments, is far more important to consider than pure research for the educator in the field. The rigid procedure of examining minute elements is the business of the researcher, not the practitioner. We may be only a decade or so away from developing basic research skills to give increased data about the intricacies of the instructional process. Until this new day arrives, we are bound to base our action on our reason and the subjective evaluations of participants in innovative programs.

When research interest quickens, and it seems bound to, it may be wise for the research studies to be carried on by a cadre of specialists who are not a part of the operation of the schools. Cold objectivity is more likely to fill the scene when there is neither personal identification or intimate familiarity with the situation being studied.

### Improvement Resources Are at Hand

Dr. Robert Garvue of Indiana University has wisely made the point that all the resources a school needs to improve its own program are at hand. Researchers have an important place in education, but this position is not one of dictation as to how a school should organize for learning. The researchers can give valuable insights into how adolescents learn, how information is internalized, and how a hundred other elements contribute to the whole of behaving, but no researcher can spell out the universally ideal organizational pattern for learning.

It is the faculty in every school that must make operational decisions to arrive at the best method of teaching for that situation. What is best in one community may not be the formula for another. Here again is an advantage of IndiFlexS. The administrator can work with his staff in shaping an organization for instruction which will bring out the best in the faculty for the maximum advantage of the students in a given school. IndiFlexS identifies a series of elements about which alterations can be made, but it does not project a rigid pattern from which sensible deviation for each school situation is scorned.

The solution to the problem of providing increased quality in instruction is a multidimensional one. Single element solutions do not solve such problems. Important as these may be—adding more teachers, purchasing more materials and supplies, changing graduation requirements, or even increasing or decreasing course requirements —they will not bring about the ultimate improvement needed in the schools. On the other hand, the variation of teaching assignments, different uses of pupil time, and rearrangement of content will go a long way toward getting the demanding job done. The schedule itself does nothing more than make it possible, maybe even likely, that teachers will make decisions and free students to achieve the goal of personalizing learning. The flexible schedule is like a new tractor. Ownership alone does not insure that the farm's yield will be increased. The tractor can make it possible for the farmer to get the job done more effectively if he uses it as it is intended. Effort is an important ingredient in almost any success.

When a school faculty makes the decision as to whether or not it is interested in employing a flexible schedule, first consideration should be given to evaluating the experiences of other educators who have employed this device. Then the literature should be surveyed to see what clues it has for arranging the various alternatives into a workable pattern for each unique situation. There is no reason for the faculty of one school to make the same errors or suffer from apprehension other practitioners have experienced.

The literature on new methods of teaching is growing in volume and in richness. A full shelf of materials is available on team teaching, small-group instruction, independent study, and technological aids to learning. All of these are valuable resources to the teaching staff considering flexible scheduling. The bibliography in this book is intended to highlight some of the significant and representative literature.

### New Work—Not Less

Those who think a flexible schedule will automatically reduce a teacher's work load err. Experience has shown teachers work as hard, if not harder, with a flexible schedule, according to the reports of the teachers at Ridgewood High in Norridge, Ilinois. However, the increased satisfaction the staff gets compensates for the added work load, the teachers seem to feel. Teachers who like their work and gain satisfaction from their efforts are usually the last to be sensitive to the teaching demands, so long as they are not unreasonable. One teacher from California reported:

> The flexible schedule has changed my whole notion of teaching. If anything, I am more interested in my students than I was with the seven period schedule. With this new interest and familiarity comes a lot of work. I spend time getting materials for individuals as well as groups but the greatest increase in time comes from the time I spend with my students individually. As I get to know my students, I can be of more help to them. This all takes time and effort.

In flexible-scheduled schools teachers participate in new activities and in traditional activities to an increased extent. They spend part of the school day in meetings with teachers, they have individual conferences with students, and they concentrate on special phases of the teaching process. At the same time, some of the deadening repetition is taken out of their work. The day is still a full one, but it is filled with varied activities and new challenges. Any evaluation of the school's schedule is incomplete if it does not center attention on the teacher's feelings toward their professional work and personal satisfaction.

During the first two years of the use of a flexible schedule at Lakeview High School, Decatur, Illinois, a careful check was kept on student and teacher attitudes toward the new organization. Results clearly indicate that the schedule must meet with favor by a vast majority of both students and teachers if it is to be successful.

The debate will go on for some time as to whether students should like their instructional activities. The weight of the argument is on the side of those who maintain students should enjoy the way their classes meet. Education should be a pleasant series of satisfying experiences. IndiFlexS assumes more learning will take place if students have positive reactions to the class structure. Therefore, an evaluation of attitudes is of concern on this issue. This kind of pulse-taking is good to do from time to time as a staff goes into a flexible schedule and after it has been involved for a period of several years.

The Brookhurst Junior High School teachers in Anaheim, California, tended to agree that students were learning as much, and in some cases more, than when the school had the timeworn schedule. A careful check was kept on the standardized test results. Brookhurst School students were doing as well, if not slightly better, under the flexible schedule than with their traditional order of classes. The staff lamented the fact these tests did not measure attitudes toward learning and interest in school. On these two factors the students would have done, the administrators felt, considerably better with the flexible schedule. The objectives of this school's program included an increased development of independent student responsibility for learning. This could not be measured by any subject-matter-oriented standardized test. Other measures need to be devised to see how well the program is meeting this objective.

The project coordinator, Dr. Ray Carlson, at Marshall High School in Portland, Oregon, reports:

> We are constantly evaluating our program and the student reactions to it. Our first survey, a random sample, indicated that eighty-six per cent were very well pleased with the program. Today I believe that most students are making a fine adjustment to their independent study time, but this is an area we constantly try to improve.

## Evaluations Before the Fact

Before a flexible schedule is inaugurated, it should be a cardinal procedure in every school to make a careful staff evaluation to see if there is acceptance of the implied assumptions of the concept. Without this acceptance by the staff and a commitment to flexible scheduling by the administration, there is every reason to believe the school program will receive little advantage. Perhaps it will be even disadvantaged.

The old saw that says "He who is convinced against his will is of the same opinion still" has application. A staff should agree to give the flexible schedule a sincere and actual chance before any adjustments are made. Evaluations of staff attitudes should be made periodically as the program is developed. These are keen guides as to the pace a school should keep in making the program change.

While there are hundreds of schools tinkering with some form of flexible schedule, others are carefully investigating and getting widespread staff understanding and commitment to the notion before any implementation will take place. Procedures for implementation have already been considered, but here it is helpful to underscore the need for an evaluation of the staff's willingness to go into a flexible schedule after the program possibilities have been discussed and all the alternate courses of action have been considered. A coordinated first step makes the succeeding ones easier and firmer. A poor start or sloppy efforts by a few teachers at varying class size are certain to have adverse influence on the total staff.

## Getting Started

One of the best ways to introduce the ideas involved in the flexible scheduling concept is to conduct a local evaluation of the school and its program. When a school staff sees itself in terms of dropouts, in terms of an accurate assessment of student mental abilities, and in terms of the use it is making of its professional talents, there is often an impetus to consider seriously the flexible-scheduling concept. While convention speeches, journal articles, and books like this may help convince people of the value of flexible scheduling, the critical moment in making a choice as to whether or not to employ the concept will come when the staff looks at its school population and its teaching performance and contrasts it with the promises of flexible scheduling. Searching appraisals of what is or is not taking place in a school are a fundamental professional duty of every school staff. The judgment of the staff in each school is the best measure of whether or not team teaching, programmed learning, flexible scheduling, or any other innovation has a place in offering even better learning and teaching opportunities.

# PART III

# STEPS WHICH MAKE MILEAGE

## CHAPTER 8

# The Task of Scheduling a School

WHILE EDUCATIONAL GOALS and content selection are most important in an educator's consideration, careful attention also must be given to the ordering of the school day and week to accomplish ultimate purposes. The school's organization for learning needs to be compatible with the objectives of the program of instruction. The instructional objectives and the requirements of content mastery should determine (1) the duration, (2) the frequency, and (3) the size of the learning group in every course. Therefore, decisions need to be made by the staff about these three matters for each course offered in the school. Until these decisions are made, an effective master schedule cannot be built.

A second set of early decisions are related to the deployment of human resources. Decisions need to be made on what parts of the instructional process each teacher on the staff will perform. This involves matching a teacher's professional strengths with the various functions to be performed in the instructional program.

The person who constructs the master schedule has a vital influence on what teachers and students can and cannot do in a school. There are important steps and critical decisions which must be established before the mechanics of scheduling begin. If these decisions are not made as an exercise of rational choice, some choices will be made by convenience, expediency, or chance. Hopefully, the individual responsible for actually ordering the master schedule will do so after taking the teaching staff into counsel.

## Sequence Is Vital

The sequence of operations presented here reports a successful way to construct the master schedule. The sequence in which these decisions are made is critical. If an administrator varies from this path, he may have to retrace his steps and redo some of the work previously done. The school schedule is like a cobweb. If one side is altered, the whole construct is changed. The consequences of these changes may mean an impossible obstacle is created. For instance, by changing an assembly group's position on the schedule after inquiry groups are set in place, conflicts between the two are nearly certain to result, then students will not be able to take the desired courses or be in the sections which conform to the teachers' specifications.

The following information is needed before the schedule can be ordered:

1. A list of each course to be offered needs to be made, including the number of inquiry and assembly groups called for each day of the week.
2. The number of students electing each course and assigned to each special section must be tabulated.
3. The number of sections of inquiry groups for each course is then determined, conforming to the specifications developed by the teaching staff.
4. The number of rooms available for each specialized facility in each content area needs to be specified.
5. The sequential arrangement of meetings per week required for each size learning groups must be indicated.
6. The length of each learning group, determined by its purpose, needs to be stated.

## First Things First

It is significant to note that student course elections are determined first. Teacher preferences then are matched to the student elections.

In a traditional schedule the procedure is often reversed. Teacher availability is settled first, and students are then assigned to the group according to the dictates of these decisions. This deviation from traditional scheduling practice is necessary if the importance of student preference is held in higher value than the assignment of teachers' time. IndiFlexS places priority on student elections and groupings; then teacher preferences are made as to the time they teach and, sometimes, what groups they instruct.

Admittedly, it is easier to put the teacher assignment on the schedule first and then match student elections to this arrangement. However, with this procedure there will be many conflicts, situations in which student course elections cannot be matched to the time when desired courses are taught. Thus, the flexible schedule puts a high priority on the need for students to be organized into groups according to learning group specifications rather than according to clerical convenience. It is difficult to justify disregarding the counselor-student determination of what courses a student should take in the name of administrative expediency. It does little good for teachers to spend time establishing learning-group specifications if they are to be disgarded in the final scheduling construction. Therefore, the learning groups are settled first.

### Essential Data Compilation

The data required in the list given above is supplied best to the administrator by the guidance and the department or division heads. These people should be responsible for making recommendations about the six topics listed. In summary form the compiled information might look like this:

| Column 1 | 2 | 3 | 4 | 5 | 6 |
|---|---|---|---|---|---|
| Course | Enroll-ment | Number of Sections | Special Room Require-ment | Meetings per Week | Modules per Meeting |
| Art I | 90 | | | | |
|    Assembly Group | 90 | 1 | | 2 | 1 |
|    Inquiry Group | 10 | 9 | A102 | 2 | 3 |
| Art II | 75 | | | | |
|    Medium Group | 20 | 4 | A104 | 2 | 4 |

| Column 1 | 2 | 3 | 4 | 5 | 6 |
|---|---|---|---|---|---|
| Course | Enroll-ment | Number of Sections | Special Room Require-ment | Meetings per Week | Modules per Meeting |
| Art III | 65 | | | | |
|   Assembly Group | 60 | 1 | | 1 | 1 |
|   Inquiry Group— Acc. | 5 | 1 | A104 | 1 | 7 |
|   Inquiry Group— Reg. | 10 | 6 | A102 or A104 | 2 | 4 |

. . . and so forth for all courses offered

FIGURE ELEVEN

Figure Eleven gives a tabulation of the class requirements for three art courses. Column One gives the course titles and indicates by the number at the right the total enrollment in the course. In the case of Art I, there are ninety enrolled students. The total beside the assembly group in Column Two gives the number to be scheduled in the assembly group. The number beside the inquiry group gives the greatest number to be in any one inquiry group. Column Three reveals the number of sections needed to schedule all the students in the course. Column Four calls attention to the special facilities required to teach the course in question. In Column Five the number of times the various sized groups meet each week is given. In Art I, for example, the teachers here asked that there be two assembly groups and two inquiry groups. The length of each of these meetings is indicated in Column Six. In Art I the assembly groups meet for one module or for thirty minutes each time and the inquiry groups meet for three connected modules or for one hour and a half each time they meet.

In this list, note that there are sixty-five students enrolled for credit in Art III. However, there are only sixty who are to be scheduled in the assembly group. Five students enrolled in this course, for unique reasons determined by the staff, are to be in one small group and will not need to attend the assembly classes. A designation Acc. has been put by their inquiry group to indicate this section is for accelerated students. Other designation letters will specify different group requirements. Furthermore, the specifications set up by the art teachers for these students indicates that the course must meet in room A104. Special facilities are in this room that demand the course be taught here. No room requirements are established for the large groups. The principal or the person doing the scheduling will work these in where feasible. Any one of the school's assembly-group facilities will work satisfactorily. So there are no requirements established by the teachers.

Perhaps it will be helpful to interpret the recommendations for other courses in this summary. In Art II there will be seventy-five students in four sections with two class sessions each week. And in Art III there will be one assembly-group class and one inquiry-group class for the accelerated small group, but there will be two inquiry sessions each week for the regular Art III students.

In every case in this list only one module for assembly-group classes is called for; but the length of the inquiry group varies from three modules, one hour and a half, to eight modules, four hours. The purpose and the methods of instruction for each course dictate the distribution of time, the kind of group to be used, and the student grouping procedures involved.

The IndiFlexS cycle is the week. Therefore, each day within the week may have a different schedule than all other days in the week, but the schedule will repeat itself each week. The total time spent in class instruction by art students in Figure Eleven, then, each week is summarized in Figure Twelve.

SELECTED SUMMARY OF GROUP MEETINGS

| Art I | | | Art II | | |
|---|---|---|---|---|---|
| Assembly Group | 1 | hour | Assembly Group | 0 | hour |
| Inquiry Groups | 3 | hours | Medium Group | 4 | hours |
| Total | 4 | hours per week | Total | 4 | hours per week |

| Art III | | | | | |
|---|---|---|---|---|---|
| Assembly Group | ½ hour | | Assembly Group | 0 | hour |
| Inquiry Group—R | 4 | hours | Inquiry Group—A 3½ | | hours |
| Total | 4½ hours per week | | Total | 3½ hours per week | |

FIGURE TWELVE

The amount of time a student spends on a subject is not determined by the amount of time he is in assembly and inquiry-group classes alone. To calculate the total time a student actually spends in a course, independent study time must be considered. In the courses given above, it is assumed students will spend time in independent study during the regular school day in each course. The teachers considered this when the various time requests were made for each course. More formal class time, however, will be spent in Art III, for example, than in Art I or Art II. The amount of time spent in independent study may vary from one week or part of the year to the next. Sometimes students will work on a single independent study project involving several content or course areas. The exact amount of time a student spends on a course cannot be determined accurately or precisely. The fused curriculum then becomes a reality!

Another category of class may be included by the staff other than assembly and inquiry groups. That is, there is no dogma that dictates classes are only to be either large (over fifty to three hundred students) or small (from seven to fifteen students). Classes can be called for by the staff of medium size. It may make more sense for some classes in art, for example, to meet in sizes which will be set by the number of stations in the room. The instructional procedures do not involve either content presentations or discussions but are centered around supervised work. Such was the case in Art III in Figure Eleven. If students are not going to discuss, but the purpose of the meeting is to paint, why should the group size be limited? The concept of variability does not imply that the options are restricted to any one or two group sizes. The methods of instruction to be used, bounded by the learning objective for the group, help the teacher judge the size of the learning group. Group sizes are merely the manifestation of how the teacher is going to order the methods of instruction available.

### Frequency and Duration Vary

The frequency and duration of learning groups will vary from subject area to subject area and from course to course. The skill courses (typing, metals, foods, etc.) will require longer sessions but fewer meetings each week than the academic courses. Some laboratory courses in science will operate similarly to the skill courses.

Courses in foreign languages which benefit from daily use of the language will meet each day, sometimes, perhaps, for only one module for drill in the language laboratory. However, they will not require lengthy sessions but daily meetings. On other days the foreign language classes may be of two or three modules, depending on the methods of instruction to be employed.

In music courses vocal groups often meet for only one module, while instrumental classes meet for three or four modules. The vocal groups can often accomplish their goal with shorter meetings causing little strain to the delicate vocal chords, while the instrumental classes need time for a great deal of repetition and group work. Some music teachers will ask for the total band to meet three times a week and for sections of the total band to meet independently one or more times per week. In these sessions the teacher can work with individuals and inquiry groups in a way that is impossible when the whole instrumental group meets. Here again the staff set up the specifications for the courses based on their judgment as the most effective way to meet with students. Examples of this variation can be cited in nearly every content area.

Appendix Two gives a model distribution of time for each course in an IndiFlexS junior-senior high school. The power of the concept would be lost if this model were adopted as a package without careful study and agreement on each decision in the proposal.

### The First Steps

The first steps in the construction of the master schedule as given in the preceding section of this chapter need to be considered in their total relationship to one another. That is, each element must be studied in relation to its effect when combined with the other elements. Once each element has been considered independently, decisions are again made that develop a sequence and pattern for each course. It would be fallacious to consider the length of class sessions without adequate thought as to the number of weekly meetings and to the amount of independent study which should be the consequence of class work. Each of the considerations summarized in Figure Eleven will be studied by the administrator once they are firmly recommended by the departments. The teaching faculty will make the determination of courses to be ·taught and the pattern of class meetings. The guidance staff will be charged with assembling the student elections. Both the teachers and guidance counselors will determine the inquiry-group specifications.

## Judgment and Feasibility

Once the teacher's recommendations and student elections are summarized in companion form as shown in Figure Eleven, they need to be evaluated by the administrator for feasibility. The administrator is ultimately responsible for all that goes on in the school. He can and should seek faculty recommendations on most matters and on nearly all involving the school's organization for learning. However, this does not mean that all requests or recommendations can be satisfied exactly. Final judgment of the distribution of the school's resources of time and faculty talent is the principal's. He is both accountable to his total faculty and responsible to his own professional judgment. If any recommendation which has been made is not, in the principal's judgment, in the finest interests of the students or staff involved, he has an obligation to question and ultimately veto the recommendation. However, it is imperative that the faculty concerned be consulted before any adjustments are made. It is devastating to a teacher's morale to be asked for a recommendation, to hear nothing about it, and finally to find the suggestion has ben ignored in favor of an alternate option. Questions, if any, should be asked by the administrator of the teacher(s) who made the particular recommendation. Usually during such meetings agreement is reached which adds to the respect of both administrator and teacher, each for the other.

The matter of feasibility should not be ignored. While the people who make recommendations have been urged to keep unavoidable bounds in mind, this sometimes does not happen. For example, a school may have only three large-group stations. With a fifteen-module day this means there are two hundred and twenty-five possibilities to use these three rooms in a week. If one room happens to be the cafeteria, it cannot be used during the lunch hours or during the preparation and cleanup time. Therefore, it is not feasible to suggest a number of large groups which is greater than the stations in which large groups can be adequately accommodated. Of course, the same concerns need to be considered for inquiry-group rooms, laboratories, and specialized independent study facilities. Thus, facility use is one important consideration to keep in mind when looking at the feasibility of schedule recommendations.

Another consideration is related to the number of modules in the week required for group meetings. Obviously it is not wise to call for more periods of instruction than are in the day for any student. However, this is not likely to happen if the inherent importance of independent study in the flexible schedule is kept in mind by the teachers. Learning, according to the assumptions made in using IndiFlexS, requires individual involvement in tasks outside of assembly and inquiry groups. Independent study is a necessary undertaking for all students in almost every course. If students are expected to spend a considerable amount of time in independent study, the problem cited here should not even develop. One of the purposes of IndiFlexS is to free students from group harnessing and give them control of and opportunity for the use of their own time. Each segment of time left for independent study makes the individual schedule that much easier to order.

Staff feasibility cannot be ignored either. More instructional groups cannot be requested than the available number of teachers can meet in a week or in a stipulated sequence. It is an easy matter to determine the total staff requirements of the flexible schedule from the form suggested in Figure Eleven. This can be done department by department. The first step is to add up the number of large-group classes called for each week. This is determined by multiplying the number of meetings per week (Column Five) by the number of modules per meeting (Column Six). Then, the number of compensation modules given must be added. The compensation modules are the blocks of added preparation time given to each teacher who makes assembly presentations. This is additional time for study, planning, media preparation, and materials selection. The suggested IndiFlexS formula was given in Figure Nine.

To finish the feasibility study of faculty requirements, the administrator needs to find out the number of teacher modules needed, again department by department, for inquiry or small groups. This is done by the same first step of procedure as mentioned for the assembly groups with an additional consideration. The number of sections is now significant. Therefore, to find out small-group teacher requirements an administrator multiplies the number of sections for each course by the number of modules per meeting by the number of meetings each week. This total gives the number of modules teachers are needed within each department each week.

This needs to be contrasted with the total number of available modules for each department staff. The assumptions made about staff time, as noted in Chapter 5, stated:

1. All teachers should have ten preparation modules each week.
2. In addition, each teaching team should meet at least one hour during the school week; other meetings may be scheduled as agreed by the team.
3. Also, each assembly group teacher should have two modules of preparation for each module of presentation.
4. Each department head should have adequate time for department duties.
5. Finally, some teachers may be given additional time for special projects or activities that are arranged to give special help to students who deviate from the norm in abilities or interests.

The total modules requested, it is obvious but worthwhile to mention, for instructional groups cannot be greater than the number of available modules of staff time for group meetings.

Imagination fails to suggest a situation in which a school staff would call for more group modules than time available if the total power of the flexible schedule has been realized. When staff recommendations for instructional groups outstrip the availability of a well-staffed school,[1] the rationale of IndiFlexS has not been accepted. If this happens the administrator needs to reassess the steps taken by the staff in their consideration and study of the flexible scheduling concept.

Once facilities, time, student elections, and teacher loads have been assessed, the feasibility study of the schedule has been completed. At this point, the administrator has made value judgments and made a feasibility analysis of the recommendations submitted. It is now time to frame a rough draft of the schedule.

CHAPTER 9

# Data-Gathering Processes

ONCE THE RECOMMENDATIONS have been made by the staff concerning the content and methods of instruction and after the faculty requests have been summarized and reviewed by the principal, the next step is to begin ordering these recommendations into a workable weekly schedule. The traditional scheduling procedure begins by generating the master schedule, and then the pupil requests are framed into the master schedule. The IndiFlexS system gathers student data, sets up group specifications, and then generates the master schedule.

Often the administrator of the traditionally scheduled school will move courses or change teaching assignments in an attempt to match students' requests to the independently determined master schedule. The process of juggling and redistributing classes in the master schedule is both a time-consuming and unsatisfactory operation. Frequently students cannot study subjects or are in sections that are selected by necessity rather than priority, even after the juggling and redistribution of the master schedule has taken place a number of times. Often as a single adjustment is made to rectify one problem or conflict, another one or even a dozen conflicts result. The school's schedule is a complex mosaic. Each student election and teacher request is a delicate piece which must be harmonized within the framework of available resources of time and facilities. Rather than determining the form and forcing pieces into it, the IndiFlexS model begins with an analysis of the pieces and then the form or the schedule is constructed.

If the person who constructs the school's schedule does not take care in getting accurate and complete input data for the scheduling process, the output cannot be expected to be precise and faultless. There will be an ultimate time savings if adequate time is spent in assembling the student and faculty data in an exact and easy to manipulate form. As the schedule is constructed each piece needs to be laid in place with care. Each step must be finalized entirely, before the administrator goes on to the next one. Much effort and time can be conserved if there is no need to retrace steps, get new summaries, or go through a segment of the scheduling a second time.

## Faculty Data

A body of information concerning faculty availability must be assembled at the outset of the actual schedule construction process. This data needs to yield information about the faculty time available in each department for instruction, the requirements for each teacher in terms of preparation periods and conferences and preferences for teaching assignments. Such a summary is shown in Figure Thirteen. The time is expressed in modules per day with a total of seventy modules to be scheduled for each teacher. This means the week is the scheduling cycle. Every day may have a different order of activities, but each week will be the same as every other week. This creates an availability resource as the schedule is actually constructed.

The data for this form frequently comes from the teachers through the department chairmen. Of course, it is to be studied, modified where necessary, and finally approved by the principal. The requests for assignments which are made by the faculty are designated after the courses to be taught and group specifications are established. The summary of these decisions was given in Figure Eleven. The compensation modules for noncontact planning and conference time was given in Figure Nine. These compensation modules include time for planning, team meetings, and staff conferences.

FACULTY DATA

Department:_____Number of Teachers:_____

Teacher One:_____ (Name)

    1. Preparation Modules:_____modules per week
    2. Team Meetings:_____modules per week, if any
    3. Department Duties:_____modules per week
    4. Assembly Groups:_____modules per week
    5. Assembly-Group Preparation:_____modules per week
    6. Inquiry Groups:_____modules per week
    7. Medium Groups:_____modules per week
    8. Individual Instruction:_____modules per week
    9. Unscheduled:_____modules per week

Teacher Two:_____ (Name)

    1. Preparation Modules:_____modules per week
    2. Team Meetings:_____modules per week, if any
    3. Department Duties:_____modules per week
    4. Assembly Groups:_____modules per week
    5. Assembly-Group Preparation:_____modules per week
    6. Inquiry Groups:_____modules per week
    7. Medium Groups:_____modules per week
    8. Individual Instruction:_____modules per week
    9. Unscheduled:_____modules per week

    . . . and so forth for all teachers in a department

FIGURE THIRTEEN

### Handling Student Election Data

A great deal of time can be saved and student elections can be handled with relative ease if the data is reported by the counselors in a systematic manner with code numbers by all learning groups. An election sheet should be prepared for each grade level or year-in-school designation. It is helpful to have the election sheets coded by color of paper for each grade level so that they can be sorted with facility. Perhaps white paper can be used for ninth-year students, pink paper for tenth-year students, and so forth.

Each election sheet should give all of the courses offered and have an appropriate place for designating particular section membership. For example, if English for ninth-grade students is to be taught by the varying class-size pattern, the counselor needs to note which assembly group and which type of inquiry group is recommended for the student. It is necessary to give a code number to each learning group which had unique specifications. It will be easier in subsequent handling of the data to refer to code numbers rather than course titles. Also, students need not be aware of the specifications of the groups when a code number is used.

When the courses are coded, it is wise to skip ten or so numbers between each department to allow for an added course or new section additions. The course coding should be sequential and include all special sections in the school. Separate codings will be helpful for both the junior and senior high schools' courses in a combination high school. Labels tend to add confusion when they are necessarily short and incomplete in describing the rationale for group composition. Also, those schools using data processing will need these group number codes. It is expedient to get the coding done at the same time the elections are determined. Figure Fourteen gives a representative part of such a form.

INDIFLEXS ELECTION FORM

Student's Name_____Counselor_____

Year in School_____Date_____

    Students are to select the courses and the groups they would like to be in for the following semester (or year).

Art Department:

_____0001 Art I, Assembly Group

_____0002 Art I, Inquiry Group

_____0003 Art I, Inquiry Group

_____0004 Art II, Medium Group

Business Department:

_____0006 Basic Business, Assembly Group

_____0017 Basic Business, Assembly Group

_____0018 Basic Business, Inquiry Group

_____0019 General Business, Assembly Group

\_\_\_\_\_0005 Art Projects

\_\_\_\_\_0020 General Business,
Inquiry Group
\_\_\_\_\_0021 Typing, Assembly
Group

. . . and so forth for each department

FIGURE FOURTEEN

It should be noted that on this form a check needs to be made by each group within a course to which a student is assigned as the election form is filled out by the counselor. For scheduling purposes, each section a student is in, even though it may be two groups for the same course, needs to be treated as an independent element. In Figure Fourteen there are two inquiry groups for Art I, numbers 0002 and 0003. Each represents a different faculty specification. Perhaps 0002 is for students with no previous art experience and 0003 is for those with prior art instruction. There probably will be a number of sections of each of these particular kinds of groups. The division of students into sections will take place during subsequent steps. At this point, the purpose is to establish student elections, not to place students in specific sections. Often a school staff will want to send this form home for parents to sign, signifying parental knowledge of what a student is taking.

Once all the student elections and group assignments have been made, tabulations are made by the secretaries to provide the tabulation data for Figure Eleven. It is from these totals that the number of sections for each course is determined. The faculty assignments are then matched with the information as shown in Figure Thirteen, with the student elections. At this point the principal will see the number of staff needed for the recommended program. If the number of sections needed is greater than the faculty availability, more staff will be required. Conversely, if the availability of staff time is greater than the number of sections called for, there is an oversupply of teaching time.

During the first few years there may be a tendency to call for more formal class meetings than will be requested after IndiFlexS is in operation for several years. After IndiFlexS is in operation for several years the program and staff requirements will change. This is attributed to two factors. First, it takes a while for students and teachers to employ independent study in place of some class activity. Second,

teachers usually recommend more class sessions as they go into Indi-
FlexS than they will need when the program is operationally secure.
With experience this tendency will be modified. The gradual transformation from more scheduled time to less is judicious as it allows
both teachers and students to adjust to the new way of teaching and
learning.

The model distribution of time between varying sized classes is one
for a school embarking on IndiFlexS for the first time (see Appendix
Two). This example is intended to be descriptive rather than prescrip-
tive. Each school staff needs to make decisions about their teaching
methods in concert with their goals and best judgment. The example
given in Appendix Two will help visualize the variety of patterns
which a staff may recommend. In this example, the learning-group
arrangements are based on the faculty's methods of teaching each
course. Some call for more assembly groups or inquiry groups than
others. The schedule is bent to the mode of learning prescribed for
each course and for students of differing abilities and interests.

### How Important Are Conflicts?

A realistic goal of IndiFlexS is to develop a schedule which honors all
the students' choices of courses and satisfies every recommendation of
the staff for group membership. This is a big order. While it sometimes cannot be filled completely, it can be realized more readily with
IndiFlexS than with a traditional schedule. In the first place, the
IndiFlexS day, with its fifteen modules of time, allows more combinations of scheduling patterns than in a six-, seven-, or eight-period day.
In the second place, the scheduling procedure of IndiFlexS is such
that it eliminates the possibility of most conflicts by following the logic
of its procedure. A conflict results when two classes a student is to be
enrolled in meet at the same time. School administrators in the
survey which was done as a part of the development of IndiFlexS,
reported that they were satisfied with scheduling by means of data
processing. One principal said that it was the best way to schedule a
traditional schedule. With eighty-seven conflicts in his school's traditional schedule, he applauded the fact that, when a flexible schedule
procedure was used in the school of about fourteen hundred students,
no conflicts resulted. Whether a flexible schedule or a traditional
schedule is used, data processing can help reduce time spent in sched-

uling and decrease the number of conflicts. The memory capacity and the possibility of redoing the schedule over and over until the correct combination of course distribution is reached is possible with data processing to an extent the memory of one mind and time of one man could not approach.

There are those who maintain that conflicts are not a serious problem in scheduling. This view does not put value on a student being in a particular course or in a specific section of a course. Whatever combination of courses fit in a program is thought to be acceptable. Those who believe this would seem to regard the school's program of studies as composed of interchangeable parts, each equal in value and utility for every pupil. Some accept the inevitability of conflicts because of inadequate knowledge of the techniques of scheduling. Too often this year's schedule is only a modification of last year's schedule. For this reason most traditionally scheduled schools do not give attention to the formulation of specifications for sections within a course. This proposition is rejected in the IndiFlexS model. Each student's elections and the new specifications for sections developed by the staff every year are the zenith of importance as the schedule is constructed.

If counselors are to spend time with students in personal program planning and if teachers are asked to gear their instruction to the capabilities and interests of students, the schedule should accommodate these professional decisions. The IndiFlexS model lays stress on the importance of individual program planning and on customized teaching. Any conflicts with what a teacher feels is the best learning arrangement or with what a student elects are considered a serious transgression of the goal of individualizing instruction. It does little good to have counselors spend hours with students if the decisions reached are not translated into the program used in the school.

The added time it takes to develop a conflict-free schedule is worthwhile in terms of ultimate student advantage. The IndiFlexS procedure will help eliminate these abridgments on student and teacher choices.

## The Conflict Analysis

If the scheduling procedure begins with the placement of learning groups on the master schedule without an assurance that students or teachers will be free to meet these groups without duplicate assignment, there is every likelihood that conflicts will result. On the other hand, if the person constructing the master schedule handles the student and teacher requests for class groups in such a way that information is obtained about the number and location of conflicts, they may be eliminated as the master schedule is finally ordered. This analysis of trouble spots is done by the use of a conflict matrix. The conflict matrix gives a comprehensive view in a systematic fashion of all the elections of students and allows the implication of teacher assignments to be seen with clarity.

The construction of the conflict matrix is a time-consuming but helpful step in the development of a sound schedule. It is a required step for developing IndiFlexS. Once the conflict matrix is mechanically set up, it can be completed by a secretary or noncertified aide. There is little reason to devote valuable administrative time to the operation of its mechanics.

The conflict matrix supplies invaluable aid in generating the master schedule. It is the guide to placement of courses and sections on the master schedule. To ignore the development of a matrix is to invite conflicts and confusion in succeeding steps of schedule construction. Data processing can be of assistance in handling the chore of constructing the conflict matrix with dispatch and ease, as with the other steps in schedule construction process. It can be constructed by hand, however.

Figure Fifteen gives an elementary view of the conflict matrix. The top line gives a code number for each learning group which has a unique set of specifications. Each number represents a course or a learning group. That is, number 001 may represent Art I, assembly group. Number 002 represents Art I, inquiry group. If there are several inquiry groups, each with unique specifications, a different number needs to be assigned to each unique specifications group. On the other hand, the conflict matrix is not concerned with limiting class size or with determining the numbers of similar inquiry or assembly groups called for in the schedule. The consideration of number of sections needed will be dispatched after the conflict matrix's usefulness has been exhausted.

Courses that are organized in one section without assembly and inquiry groups have only one number. For instance, if students in Art II were to meet in one class group, then there would be only one number on the top line of the conflict matrix, Number 003. At the same time, if all students in a course are to be in both assembly and inquiry groups, but there are no particular specifications for the inquiry groups, then only one number is needed in the top line of the conflict matrix to handle these elections. This will be the situation in some courses where there are no unique specifications for the various inquiry groups.

A conflict matrix should be developed for each grade level in the school. To put all the elections of the school's entire population on one conflict matrix would be a difficult clerical chore. Also, the master schedule will be generated on a grade-level by grade-level basis, and the matrix will be referred to on a grade-by-grade basis.

The numbers in the left column are matched with the numbers on the top line. The encircled numbers found on the diagonal from left to right give the total number enrolled; the numbers in each cell match courses elected by a student. When there is no conflict between courses, only one entry is made in the diagonal column.

It will be helpful to put a circle around the assembly group numbers on the top line. This will be useful at a later stage of the scheduling process. The system described represents a departure from the conflict sheet often used to build a traditional schedule.

CONFLICT MATRIX

|   | 001 | 002 | 003 | 004 | 005 | 006 |
|---|---|---|---|---|---|---|
| 001 | ③ 111 | 11 | 1 |   | 11 | 111 |
| 002 |   | ② |   |   | 1 |   |
| 003 |   |   | ① |   |   | 1 |
| 004 |   |   |   | ④ |   | 1 |
| 005 |   |   |   |   | ③ |   |
| 006 |   |   |   |   |   | ⑤ |

FIGURE FIFTEEN

The following data will help in the interpretation of Figure Fifteen:

Group 001: Art I course, assembly group, three students enrolled to date

Group 002: Art I course, inquiry group for students of a particular grouping criteria, perhaps the talented art students, two students enrolled to date

Group 003: Art I course, inquiry group for students of another grouping classification, perhaps for those without previous art instruction, one student enrolled to date

Group 004: Basic Business course, all students enrolled in a traditionally sized class, four students enrolled to date

Group 005: Salesmanship course, all students in both assembly and inquiry classes, three students enrolled to date

Group 006: English course, assembly group, five students enrolled to date

The conflict matrix as shown in Figure Fifteen indicates that the following distribution of elections yields the conflicts given: 2 are in 001 and 002; 1 is in 001 and 003; 2 are in 001 and 005 and 3 are in 001 and 006. There are no conflicts with 001 and 004. This means that all of the five students scheduled to date are in all of the courses except 004 (Basic Business). Group 001 ( Art I, assembly group) can be scheduled the same time as group 004, Basic Business. Of the two students in group 002, one also is in group 005 (Salesmanship) and all are in group 006 (English, assembly group). Therefore, group 002 cannot be scheduled during the modules that groups 005 and 006 meet, but can be scheduled as far as student availability is concerned during the modules groups 003 and 004 meet.

An entry is made along the left column each time a student's election is recorded. This gives the course tally of total enrollments in each group or course. This total will be the basis for determining the number of sections needed for each course. Also, each time a student is taking the course or is enrolled in a section, an entry is made in the appropriate cell, reading from the top down. At a glance the number of students signed up for the same course can be readily seen. Therefore, when placements are made in the master schedule of each course, the conflict matrix is a guide as to when sections can be properly placed.

### Special Course Placement

Once the conflict matrix is completed consideration can be given to special placement of courses at critical times in the day. For example, sometimes teachers request scheduling foods classes in the homemaking department during the lunch hours so the students can sample their food or prepare full-course meals. Classes that rely heavily on out of school field trips may be scheduled at the beginning or end of the day to accommodate the travel students need to do.

Youngsters with limited attention spans may profit from being scheduled into academic courses in the morning when there is less likelihood of fatigue. Students in vocational programs where they are on the job for part of the day need to be identified before the course or section assignments are made.

Some teachers may only be in the building for part of the day due to service in other buildings or because they are part-time teachers. At this point in the process it is necessary to study each department and identify these special provisions that need to be honored. Once these matters have been studied, it is time to begin putting the master schedule together.

## CHAPTER 10

# Generation of the Master Schedule

Because of the previous steps taken in gathering the data about student elections and teacher prescriptions, the actual generation of the master schedule will not be a perplexing task. Yet it will be time-consuming and require countless decisions about important instructional matters. During this stage of the process teachers will be matched with student groups, specific assignments of time will be made to each learning group, and class groups will be established in cases not specified by the counselors and teachers.

*Teachers First*

The first items put on the master schedule will be the required teachers' meetings and conferences. However, general teacher-planning periods will not be assigned until all the class meetings are put on the schedule. The conferences put on the schedule at this point are (1) department head meetings, (2) team meetings, and (3) any special time given to teachers for specific purposes such as audiovisual direction, attendance officer's work, and the like.

Some schools may want to attempt to schedule one team meeting a week and the department heads' meeting before or after a lunch module. This allows these groups to eat together. Where there are separate dining rooms, these meetings sometimes extend through the lunch hour. Of course, all of these meetings cannot be assigned then since a third of the school's classes will need to be in session during each lunch module.

## Lunch Time

IndiFlexS provides for three lunch sessions during the sixth, seventh, and eighth modules. Students and teachers will be eating in three groups. They may not eat during the same module each day. In schools that span six years, a strict division of lunch assignments will probably be made. Junior high students will eat at one time, senior high students at another. Such requirement places a mild restriction on the mobility possible in the schedule.

## From Upper to Lower

As the master schedule is developed, it is expedient to begin with the highest grade level in the school. In a senior high school this step will begin with the twelfth-year students; in the junior high it will begin with the ninth-year students. This is done because the most divergent course requests likely will be in these two grades. Students in the upper years tend to take more elective subjects, and there is a tendency for the faculty's grouping specifications to be more detailed in the upper years.

In the senior high school some twelfth-year students may be taking vocational courses—distributive or office occupations and distributive education—which will require that they be out of the building part of the day. This means that preference is required for seniors in setting the times of the courses they will take.

It is wise to schedule all the students on one grade level at a time for another reason as well. It will be easier to remember all of the vital factors for one grade level at one time than to attempt to keep certain restrictions in mind for all three or four grade levels. For example, perhaps the teacher who teaches ninth-year homemaking is only available half days. Or the junior year physical education program may need to meet in the afternoon to accommodate those juniors who are in the morning vocational program. Also, one teacher may need to teach certain groups in the morning for one reason or another. All of these special qualifications must be kept in view and it is less difficult to do it if one group is being dealt with at a time. When the highest grade level in the school is scheduled, it is appropriate to move down to the next highest grade until all the school is scheduled.

## Out of Sequence

Some students will be out of their grade-level sequence, when they are taking courses that are not usually taken by students on their grade level. Some pupils may be taking advanced courses; some upperclassmen may be taking some courses with underclassmen. As the use of IndiFlexS is extended, hopefully more and more students will fall in this category.

These students' election sheets should be pulled out of their grade-level group and scheduled course by course with the grade level on which the course is usually taken. For example, a sophomore taking the third year of language should have his language course scheduled with the juniors. Then when this is accomplished his election sheet should be returned to the sophomore group for the completion of his schedule when the sophomores are scheduled.

## From Large to Small

Classes will be assigned to the master schedule beginning with the assembly groups and going to the inquiry groups on each grade level. If a conflict results necessitating moving a class meeting time, it is often easier to move an inquiry group of seven to fifteen students than to move an assembly class.

Once all the assembly groups are scheduled on each grade level, the single section medium-size groups are put in place. Within this category preference should be given to the medium-size groups which meet five days a week. Then those that meet less than five days should be set in place. It is important to remember that classes that meet five days a week do not have to meet at the same time each day. The complexities of IndiFlexS will probably not make the same meeting times each day possible.

Next the extended length inquiry groups, those that meet for more than two modules, should be put on the master schedule. The last groups to be scheduled are the two-module and one-module inquiry groups.

As each group is put on the master schedule, it should be checked off the work sheet shown in Figure Eleven. This will assure the assignment of each learning group to the master schedule.

## Master Schedule Form

It will be necessary to make the master schedule in a way that gives each teacher a page which has cells for the five days and fifteen modules for each day. This is shown in Figure Sixteen. When the master schedule is complete, it will be reproduced so that each teacher's schedule is on a separate page.

The schedule is organized so that when it is put in final booklet form, it begins with the art teacher(s) and gives the teachers' schedules in each department in alphabetical order. For easy reference it

TEACHER'S MASTER SCHEDULE PAGE

| Teacher's Name: | Department: | | | Page: | |
|---|---|---|---|---|---|
| Module | Monday | Tuesday | Wednesday | Thursday | Friday |
| 1 | | | | | |
| 2 | | | | | |
| 3 | | | | | |
| 4 | | | | | |
| 5 | | | | | |
| 6 | | | | | |
| 7 | | | | | |
| 8 | | | | | |
| 9 | | | | | |
| 10 | | | | | |
| 11 | | | | | |
| 12 | | | | | |
| 13 | | | | | |
| 14 | | | | | |
| 15 | | | | | |

FIGURE SIXTEEN

is helpful to add a contents page which lists the faculty in alphabetical order and designates the page on which each schedule is to be found.

When the schedule is constructed by the hand method, the control of teacher assignment is done by the single sheet for each teacher. It is impossible to assign two groups to one teacher at one time when the teacher's master schedule page shows previous assignments or modules already used.

The information about the teachers' requests for assignment was determined earlier and recorded on Figure Thirteen. As the principal constructs the schedule, he will consult the recommendations made by the faculty and then match them with the gross figures of student elections and assignments as given in Figure Eleven.

## Over and Over

It is best to write the master schedule assignments on the teachers' sheets in pencil so that changes can be made without redoing the entire sheet.

The person who makes the master schedule will go from page to page of the teachers' master schedule pages (Figure Sixteen), putting on the various groups. To summarize, this will be done in the following order:

1. Begin with the first teacher in alphabetical order in the art department and move through the departments in alphabetical order.
2. Place team meetings, regularly planned conferences, and other essential staff activities which require particular meeting times on the schedule.
3. Put upperclassmen's courses on first and then go down to underclassmen, including out-of-sequence students with the appropriate grade-level group.
4. Schedule assembly groups first.
5. Next put on medium-sized five-day-a-week courses.
6. Add extended module inquiry groups.
7. Next double session inquiry groups, single section classes first, are ordered.
8. Finally, assign the regular planning modules and make assign-

ments of staff for independent study projects and for consultation in the instructional materials center.

## An Aid, not a Solution

The construction of the conflict matrix did not eliminate class conflicts. However, it did identify where they would occur. The conflicts are either created or eliminated as the master schedule is generated. Therefore, frequent reference must be made to the conflict matrix before any class is assigned to the master schedule.

Before a course is placed on the master schedule, the principal will want to consult (1) the conflict matrix (Figure Fifteen), (2) the faculty teaching request form (Figure Thirteen), and (3) the student election and assignment form (Figure Eleven). The faculty data form tells the principal what teachers are available for each course. The student election and assignment form gives an exact total of the required number and type of sections to be scheduled. The conflict matrix will indicate when sections cannot be scheduled without presenting a conflict.

As the conflict matrix (Figure Fifteen) is consulted it is important to remember that certain apparent conflicts between some inquiry groups and other sections of inquiry groups are not conflicts for all students. A group of fifteen English students, for instance, may meet at the same time as another inquiry group of a dozen or so social studies students meet. There will be considerable latitude in the distribution of students to inquiry groups where all students on a grade level are in one inquiry-group section within the same subject. Inquiry groups with particular specifications cannot be scheduled without care in checking the probability of students in these courses taking other courses set for the same time.

## From Left to Right, Top to Bottom

To help insure an equal distribution of students in assembly groups at any one time, thus relieving pressures on the use of special equipment and facilities, it is wise to place the assembly groups on the schedule with an even pattern. The pattern may be to put assembly groups on beginning with the first module on Monday, the next on the first module on Tuesday, and so forth through Friday. The next module used should be the second on Monday and so on until the assembly groups are distributed through the week. This order is shown in Figure Seventeen.

| Module | Monday | Tuesday | Wednesday | Thursday | Friday |
|--------|--------|---------|-----------|----------|--------|
| 1 | 1st<br>Art I | 2nd<br>Art III | 1st<br>Art I | 1st<br>Art I | 2nd<br>Art. III |
| 2 | 3rd<br>Bas. Bus. | 4th<br>Salesman-<br>ship | 3rd<br>Bas. Bus. | 4th<br>Sales. | 3rd<br>Bas. Bus. |
| 3 | 5th<br>Typing I | 6th<br>Gen. Bus. | 5th<br>Typing I | 6th<br>Gen. Bus. | 7th<br>Bus. Law |
| 4 | 7th<br>Bus. Law | 8th<br>Eng. I | 9th<br>Speech | 8th<br>Eng. I | 10th<br>Engl. II |

. . . and so forth through the day

FIGURE SEVENTEEN

It will be necessary to place some assembly groups at one or another position in the day for special reasons, as has been noted in Chapter 9. Special time requirements should be honored first. Then the rotation scheduling can begin. When the regular turn comes for the use of modules specially scheduled, the modules used should be skipped. Also, the routine of moving from left to right and going from top to bottom on the master schedule should not be preserved at the expense of any particular request for time placement of an assembly group by a teacher. This rotation system is used merely as a guide to balancing class sizes and getting an even distribution of students in each facility.

The same routine of assigning medium-size classes and inquiry groups should be used. In addition to keeping the various facilities used on an evenly distributed basis, this will tend to scatter the assembly groups for a given student throughout the day. Thus, no student should have to go from one assembly group to another without intermittent time for inquiry group and independent study activity.

## Room Check

It will be helpful to keep a check of the use of rooms as the schedule calls for their use. Since the schedule is framed over a period of days, it is difficult to remember which rooms are already used and which are open for assignment. The form shown as Figure Sixteen can be used for this purpose. In place of the teacher's name, the room number can be inserted. As the room is used each module, a check can be made in the cell of the appropriate module to show its use. In most schools it is a waste of time to do this for inquiry-group rooms as they will not be as difficult to schedule as will the assembly-group rooms.

## Rounding out the Schedules

Once these steps have been completed and the tentative master schedule is framed for all of the learning groups, it is time to schedule the independent study groups and make assignments of teachers to the instructional materials center. Most schools will want to have a teacher from each department available in the instructional materials center each module of the day, for the reasons discussed in Chapter 6. These assignments will be made after all of the classes have been assigned. The preparation modules are the last to be added to the tentative master schedule.

The number of modules available for teachers to work on special projects or on special activities for students is determined by the staffing ratio and the number of formal learning groups required. It seems advisable to schedule some remedial and project activity for students during the early use of IndiFlexS. Unfortunately, schools using flexible scheduling have reported little use of teacher time for special project and remedial work with students. Perhaps it would be advantageous to schedule some students in these one-to-one regular sessions with teachers in the early phases of the use of IndiFlexS.

The procedure used for scheduling classes, moving from left to right and top to bottom through the weekly schedule, should be used in assigning teachers to the instructional materials center. However, preference should be given to several module blocks for planning, rather than splitting up a series of modules for consultation service in the instructional materials center.

## On a Tentative Basis

The master schedule generated at this point is in a tentative form. There may need to be adjustments of a minor nature, perhaps none will be required. Changes may be made in the schedule produced thus far after the faculty have seen it or when the student assignments are made to the sections. This process will be discussed in Chapter 11.

It is recommended that the tentative master schedule be distributed before school is dismissed or mailed to the staff in the summer for their suggestions, reactions, and comments. Often helpful suggestions can be injected which will improve the schedule. At this point, only changes of location and student composition of sections can be made. The sequence and pattern of group size should be preserved in most cases or the entire process must begin again.

The other factor which makes this a tentative schedule is the potential existence of problems which may result as the students are assigned to particular learning groups. These will be dealt with in detail in Chapter 11.

## A Schedule for Scheduling

It may be helpful to suggest a schedule for making decisions about the construction of the master schedule. This is only suggestive. Its greater value is in its sequence, rather than the dates suggested. These may vary from school to school depending on guidance procedures and budget planning dates.

SEQUENCE AND TIME TABLE FOR SCHEDULING

| Step | Task | Month |
|------|------|-------|
| First | Isolation of Particular Educational Objectives | September-October |
| Second | Selection of Courses, Content, and Learning Activities | November-December |
| Third | Determination of Instructional Mode for each Course (Class Size, Frequency, and Duration of Class Meetings, and so forth) | January-February |

| Fourth | Recommendation of Specifications for Learning Groups | January-February |
| Fifth | Accumulation of Student Tentative Elections | January-March |
| Sixth | Suggestion for Staff Assignments to Courses | February |
| Seventh | Construction of Tentative Master Schedule<br>    Assembly Groups First<br>    Medium-size Five-day-a-week Classes Second<br>    Extended Module Inquiry Groups Third<br>    Double and Single Module Inquiry Groups Fourth<br>    Completion of Faculty Assignments Fifth | April-May |
| Eighth | Assignment of Students to Learning Groups | June-July-August |

FIGURE EIGHTEEN

CHAPTER 11

# Developing Class Assignments

AFTER THE tentative master schedule has been constructed, the scheduling tasks yet to be done are largely routine clerical chores until a problem situation arises, if it does. The raw expenditure of hours is the greatest at this stage of the operation. Although some professional decisions will need to be made, most of the succeeding steps can be done by clerks.

Schools which use data processing in assigning students to their classes will be able to wait until much later to begin this phase than those which do the assignment of students to classes by hand. One of the several advantages of data processing is that it allows the administration to make election and group composition changes up until a day or so before school begins. Since the final program for each student does not have to be done until the day before school begins, the process of generating it should be delayed until the last minute. Thus, new students can be scheduled with the other students when data processing is used. When the job is done by hand, making student assignments cannot be put off until the week before school begins because of the longer length of time needed to get the operation completed.

From this point on in the process a cost analysis between the use of data processing and the hand method of scheduling is difficult to make; but it is reasonable, also verified in at least two situations, that it is less expensive to do the remaining tasks with data processing

4 0 0 0 1965

# The enlargement of the Presidency

than by the hand method. However, other unrelated clerical staff duties to be done, wage-scale differences, and working-speed variations make it difficult to arrive at cost figures for scheduling from school to school. There are few operational expenditures which are potentially any more beneficial than those for developing a schedule which is as nearly ideal as possible.

## When and Where Data Processing

In an age when yesterday's unknowns are today's knowledge, it is difficult to be up-to-date in making assertions about what technology, data processing included, can or cannot do. At this point in time, data-processing programs are useful in the scheduling process *once the master schedule is constructed*. Other than providing a conflict matrix, data processing has been of little help thus far in generating the master schedule. The time may soon come when the assistance of data processing will be available in generating the master schedule. Research in this problem is underway in at least two of the country's major universities, Stanford University and the Massachusetts Institute of Technology.

Colleges of education, state departments of public instruction, county superintendents of schools, or perhaps private service bureaus could perform an invaluable aid to the schools if they would offer complete scheduling consultation and data-processing service to all the schools in a geographic area. It is with the view of not only reducing the work load but also, and more important, of offering alternate possibilities of bringing students and teachers together in the most effective way that this service has its fullest promise. The face of American secondary education might well be changed if the scheduling considerations of the principal were to shift from clerical expediencies to calculated judgments. The financial support to get data-processing programs developed to generate a master schedule will take the massive assistance of either a foundation, a federal government grant, or a cooperative effort of several of the country's large educational or private enterprise institutions.

The computer will always be a moron. Yet it has helpful and tremendous memory storage and sorting capacity. Computers cannot make decisions, but they can sort, re-sort, and sort again data to bring about ideal arrangements of particular students and available teachers. The memory capacity of the computer goes beyond the upper limits of any man. At the same time, it will give accurate options in convenient form from properly ordered information. The principal's worth to the school as the educational leader is likely to increase when data processing is called into play. However, until the scheduling logic is programmed, its value is restricted to functioning after the master schedule is constructed.

## The Hand Versus Machine Method

Data processing will open new doors for the secondary school in this important area of schedule construction. Schools which have the resources and opportunity will find a tremendous time-saving advantage with the use of data processing.

The steps suggested for construction of the flexible schedule can be done by either hand or machine. The method presented here is geared to schools that do not have data-processing resources. What can be done by hand can also be done equally well and much faster by use of data processing.

There may be merit for a principal to do the job of constructing a master schedule by hand before using data-processing machines. The hand method gives the administrator a full understanding of the scheduling process. The student of school administration will profit from an analysis of the hand method of scheduling for the same reason.

Hopefully, all schools will soon employ data processing for schedule construction, test analysis, and a long list of other uses. The more time a machine can save the principal and his staff, the more time there is for performing tasks on a professional, nonclerical level.

Data processing will not make decisions; it will only implement them. The output data in a machine-accomplished schedule can never be better than the input data provided by the principal and the staff. That is to say, the goals must be firm, the available resource data must be expressed in an accurate and complete form, and the student input information must be precise and accurate before data-processing results will be usable.

Some schools which do not have data-processing equipment have found it profitable to employ a service bureau to do the job for them. Data-processing service bureaus can be helpful at low costs if they have the proper program for their equipment. The major data-processing companies can supply the names of service bureaus in each area of the country if a service bureau is not in the town in which the school is situated.

As a matter of caution, do not engage a service bureau unless the personnel of the bureau assures you they have both the equipment and the program to do the job. One suburban Chicago school engaged a service bureau and was in a state of panic on the first day of school in September when they found the bureau had not done the job correctly. This school, interestingly enough, did not use a flexible schedule. The fault was not the equipment's inadequacy, but the imprecision and incompleteness of the input data. The root of this problem was a breakdown in communication between the service bureau's representatives and the school principal. While the situation was rectified in a few days, the year was started on an unfortunate note of disorganization and confusion. This bureau scheduled thirteen other schools without impediment that same September. The problems then in the one school were not related to the capabilities of the machines but to communication difficulties of the people involved.

Flexible schedules present special but not insurmountable problems to data processors. Careful selection of the people who will manage the program and handle the data is the answer to the successful solution of any problems in this regard.

## The Card System

It is recommended that a card system be used to assign students to classes. A card will need to be printed for each seat that may be occupied in each learning group. A set of cards should be made for each group listed on the tentative master schedule. It is suggested that the cards be color coded, one color for assembly groups and another for inquiry groups.

There should be several more cards made than the number of students signed up for each course to serve as a cushion when new students are enrolled. Of course, at no time should there be more cards for a group than the number of students to be accommodated in the group. For example, if an inquiry class in the social studies is to have no more than nine students in each section, no more than nine cards should be printed for this section. However, some groups should be organized with extra enrollment potential to make room for students who transfer into the school or for those who change courses as the year progresses.

The cards should be arranged in open files, department by department. All of the cards should contain essential information about the group, including course title, group purpose (assembly or inquiry), the days and the modules it meets, and the teacher's name. Figure Nineteen suggests such a format.

CLASS SCHEDULE CARD—ASSEMBLY GROUP

| French I<br>Tuesday—4th Module<br>Friday—7th Module<br>Room—100A | (The student's name will<br>be added here later.) |
|---|---|

| 1st Period | 2nd Period | 3rd Period | 4th Period | Final Grade |
|---|---|---|---|---|
| | | | | |

Mr. Jones

FIGURE NINETEEN

In succeeding steps there can be no more students scheduled for a class than the number of cards available. Thus, when the cards are made, the room capacities and group sizes are limited.

These cards can be made of light paperboard stock and printed by an address-printing machine. Schools which do not already have such a machine can find one in nearly any community's newspaper office, hospital, or in some business establishments. Those who are scheduling small schools may use duplicating stencils to make these cards. Manufacturers often will either rent or sell these addressing machines for a reasonable price to schools.

These cards can also be used for reporting grades, attendance, or both. When schools use them for these purposes, other forms can be eliminated. Figure Nineteen is set up to record grades. The same card can be used for attendance reporting by printing cells for each day in the year on the back of the card. When a student is absent, a check can be made in the appropriate cell. Grades usually will be given by the inquiry-group teachers, thus the assembly-group cards may not need to record this information. Attendance may not be taken in the assembly groups but only in the inquiry groups. When this is the case, the attendance cells on the back of the two assembly cards may be ignored.

A more sophisticated class schedule card is given in Figure Twenty. This kind of card can be used for key sorting operations or for other uses in accumulating information. A grade analysis, class-size summary, and other summaries can be made from such a card.

A STUDENT SCHEDULE CARD MODEL

FIGURE TWENTY

*Matching Elections with Classes*

After all of the class cards have been made and put in the file bins, the job of matching the student elections and special group assignments to the special classes begins. Each student election sheet is used as the basis of class assignment. The person matching the elections to the specific class assignments uses the student election sheet (Figure Fourteen) as a guide to the class requirements for each student.

It has already been mentioned that it is wise to begin with the highest grade in the school and schedule these students first. This gives preference in assigning sections to the older students. In instances where students will be out of school for vocational or work programs, it is helpful to get these students assigned to classes before sections begin to fill up and the range of choice is narrowed. Also, if conflicts are still to develop, they most likely will congregate in the upper years. Adjustments can be made to resolve them.

If the clerical operation of pulling class cards to match elections yields a conflict, that particular student election card should be put aside immediately. The principal should be notified and the cause of the problem and possible solutions should be studied. It is difficult and not particularly productive to make conjectures about the cause of conflicts found during this stage. Most often they will result from errors made in recording student preferences for courses or sections. Or a mistake was made by the principal as the tentative master schedule was produced. In any case, a change needs to be made in the tentative master schedule to accommodate each student's elections. Usually this requires adjusting an inquiry-group section. Infrequently it will call for a change in an assembly-group placement on the master schedule.

It is recommended that adjustments be made on the master schedule so that every student will be in the course he elects and the kind of section to which he is assigned. This may mean considerable redoing of work already done but the value to the student in being in a particular section is inestimable. Individualized instruction requires individual scheduling for each student. Group or gang class-assigning procedures are a transgression of the principles at the foundation of flexible scheduling.

### The Matching Sequence

In using an established sequence of matching student elections with class assignments a great deal of time can be saved and any one of several worker's steps can be traced at each point in the procedure. The sequence suggested is to pull cards for all assembly groups first, for all five-day-a-week medium-sized classes second, for extended module classes third, and for all double and single module inquiry groups last. This sequence will result in making the proper selection of a section when there are several sections from which to choose. Some combinations of arrangements of sections will not fit together while others will mesh. For example, a single four-module class may meet only during the first four modules; thus a student taking this course should be in other inquiry groups which meet at other times. In this situation it saves time to take the extended module card first and then select a section for the double module class that meets after the fourth module. Failure to use this sequence will result in refiling cards and in consuming time with pulling new cards. The following sequence, then, should be used in locating the class cards for each student:

1. Pull assembly class cards,
2. Pull five-day-a-week class cards,
3. Pull extended module class cards,
4. Pull double and single module class cards.

## The Student's Schedule Card

As a card is pulled establishing the enrollment of a student in a class, a check should be made in the appropriate module on the student schedule card. The student schedule card is the form which will be given to the student to tell him where to go for each class and when each class meets. A form for this purpose is suggested in Figure Twenty-One.

Beside each module there are three lines for recording various class assignments. Since all classes will not meet for five days a week, provision is made to report different class membership for different days.

The blank space in the upper left-hand corner is used for putting in the student's name, address, phone, class standing, and parents' names. This information can be put on an address label or metal addressing plate for several uses. These will be discussed later in more detail. The information in the lower right corner will be filled in after all the scheduled classes are set in place.

Several copies of this card will be required. One copy will be given to the student. At least two others should be made, one for the general office's use and the other for the guidance department. The student's copy may be printed on paper while the other copies are more easy to file if printed on light paperboard stock. Other information which either the office or the guidance department may desire can be called for on the back of the card. Sometimes this includes birth date, number of years attended school, and other helpful information.

STUDENT SCHEDULE CARD

| Mod. | M | T | W | T | F | Course | Rm. |
|------|---|---|---|---|---|--------|-----|
| 8 |  |  |  |  |  |  |  |
| 9 |  |  |  |  |  |  |  |
| 10 |  |  |  |  |  |  |  |
| 11 |  |  |  |  |  |  |  |
| 12 |  |  |  |  |  |  |  |
| 13 |  |  |  |  |  |  |  |
| 14 |  |  |  |  |  |  |  |
| 15 |  |  |  |  |  |  |  |

| Mod. | M | T | W | T | F | Course | Rm. |
|------|---|---|---|---|---|--------|-----|
| 1 |  |  |  |  |  |  |  |
| 2 |  |  |  |  |  |  |  |
| 3 |  |  |  |  |  |  |  |
| 4 |  |  |  |  |  |  |  |
| 5 |  |  |  |  |  |  |  |
| 6 |  |  |  |  |  |  |  |
| 7 |  |  |  |  |  |  |  |

Homeroom: . . . . Bus Rider? . . .
Counselor: . . . . . . . . . . . . . . . . .

FIGURE TWENTY-ONE

A check is made in the appropriate module's cell each time a card is pulled from the class card file. The course title and room are not recorded at this point. The purpose there is to select the proper class cards. A large paper clip is put around the student-counselor election sheet (Figure Fourteen), the class cards (Figure Twenty), and the student schedule form (Figure Twenty-One). The person pulling the cards does not go on to the next student until all the cards for one student are completely selected.

The only identification of the student's class cards at this time is by reading his name on the election sheet. Therefore, it is imperative that the election sheet and class cards not be separated.

When several sections or more of one kind of group are available for assignment, it is wise to pull the cards from these sections in order. That is, if there are two or more industrial arts inquiry groups, it is not sound to fill one section and then move to the other. Instead a card for the first student to be scheduled should come from one section. When the next student is scheduled, his card should come from another section. This will tend to keep the classes balanced and, at the same time, keep places open for students whose other course combinations perhaps require being in a particular section.

It should be expected that sometimes a card may have to be pulled from a student's packet so that a section membership may be exchanged with a student who requires the other student's place in the group. For this reason names were not placed on any of the cards when the class cards were pulled from the file bins.

## Special Group Specifications

There will be little problem with the students assigned to special inquiry groups since the placement of these courses was assessed on the conflict matrix as the sections were assigned to the tentative master schedule. Also, the number of cards made for each section was taken from the teacher's request form (Figure Eleven). This gave the number of sections and the number of students to be scheduled in each course.

A problem of keeping the sections balanced and arriving at workable combinations of classes arises from multiple-section courses with single-group composition specifications. By alternating the selection of cards from these sections, difficulty in fitting schedules together without conflicts can be reduced. It should be expected that some class assignments will be more difficult to arrange than others. This means that some students' programs will have to be done a second and third time to find the right combination of arrangement of sections.

The more specific the staff gets in isolating approaches to instruction and the more that is known about students individually, the more precise the learning-group specifications will become. While there will be added time spent in putting these groups on the tentative master schedule, the task of pulling cards is easier for them because the range of choice is necessarily limited.

## The Printing Task

When all the class cards have been pulled for every student in the school, it is time to print the names on both the class cards and on the students' schedule cards. This can be done by hand or by typewriter. However, it is strongly recommended that addressing labels or an addressing machine be used on both the class cards and the student schedule cards.

The addressing machine can print the student's name, address, class, parents' name, phone number, and homeroom with one press of a lever. This information should be put on each class card (Figure Twenty), and on the student's schedule card (Figure Twenty-One). One school found it helpful to put addresses on four envelopes at the same time the cards were run through the addressing machine. These were used for mailing progress cards to parents. Student directories can also be made with ease from these plates. Each plate can be used over and over with alterations being made as needed when addresses, grade levels, or homerooms change. Of course, if data-processing procedures are used, the step in printing the schedules is done with a considerable saving of clerical time.

## Checking and Rechecking

After each name has been put on all the appropriate class and schedule cards, the student's schedule card is filled out completely. The information added to the student's schedule card includes the course title and the room in which each group meets. The time of each meeting was checked as the class cards were selected from the file bins. Filling out the schedule card involves taking the information from the class card (Figure Twenty), and putting it on the student's schedule card (Figure Twenty-One). As this information is put on the student's schedule card, the accuracy of the assignments will be checked against the class cards. Verification that no deletions have been made in the process of handling the class cards is made as the student election sheet is checked the final time.

Counselor assignment can be communicated to the student by the schedule card. During the first day of school, students make the number of copies of schedule cards needed by the administrator and counselors. Locker numbers and combinations, bus route information, and other details can be easily put on these cards also.

## Worth the Effort

It is worth the expenditure of unusual effort to get the year off to a smooth start. Therefore, it is good insurance to check the class assignments recorded on the student's schedule card to make certain that all assignments are accurate.

During the first years of the use of IndiFlexS, it might be sound procedure to begin the school year with a student assembly. During this assembly the student leaders and principal can give their greetings and the school's program can be explained by several members of the staff, each dwelling on some particular aspect of the school's organization. After this, students can report to various places throughout the building to pick up their schedules. Then the students should go to their first module classes to fill out their cards, hear other essential announcements and, most important, begin the school year. The sooner the classes begin, the easier it will be for students to get their schedules in mind and begin operating under the new procedures IndiFlexS implies.

The registration procedure is completed before students enter school for the first day. The first day of school can be the first day of class. The time spent in preregistration will be realized as advantageous on the first day of the new school year.

## Use of Class cards

After the scheduling has been completed and the student schedule card is filled out, all of the class cards should be arranged in groups according to teacher and class. That is, all of one teacher's courses should be put in a packet for each learning gorup. These packets of cards can be given to the teachers and serve as records of the membership for each class. By using these cards, class lists do not need to be made.

If students who are registered do not report for class, their cards are sent to the counselors and these people are easily dropped from the school roll. Class sizes are simply determined by taking a count of either the cards left in the file bins or those in each teacher's group.

## Add and Drop

From the first day of school through most of the school year, there may be a number of course changes. Students and teachers will want to add, drop, and change courses or sections from time to time. This can be both a helpful and bothersome process. It is helpful to the student, but sometimes bothersome to the administrator and counselor who deal with each case. Here again administrative convenience should be ignored in favor of the possible advantage to a student by a program change.

Each program change should be instituted administratively through the student's counselor. If the change is in the student's best interest, his counselor should be in a position to make the appropriate recommendation. Teachers sometimes will suggest changes in student programs. Also, in these cases the counselor should be consulted by the teacher. Once an agreement for a change has been made, the mechanics will be handled by the principal's office in the same way the original program was constructed.

The flexible scheduling rationale does not have calendarized limits. Students can shift from section to section or from course to course whenever their performance, current or potential, dictates the move is warranted. If a student would seem to profit from being in a different inquiry group, this change should be effected. Or if a student should do the work in another level course and would profit little from staying in a course, a program change should be made without question. Slow learners often realize personal advantage if they are transferred from originally assigned regular courses to courses which deal with concepts or processes more suited to the individual student.

The approach used by the counselors in dealing with individual students and the orientation of the staff toward program changes will influence the extent to which class adjustments are a benefit to a school program. Care must be taken to see that class adjustments do not carry an unwholesome stigma *or* that they become a badge for the lazy and reluctant learner. Indeed, it is lamentable when students are moved about like pawns because of the teacher's problem in sparking an interest in learning.

## Nongrading Follows

Flexible scheduling leads to a variety of new opportunities and challenges for both students and teachers. For the student it offers the opportunity to learn at his own rate, in his own universe of capability, and by his own effort. Flexible scheduling provides opportunities for education with self-direction. Questions of *what, how,* and to a lesser extent, *when* a student wants to learn are matters for individual concern and determination. The challenge to learn is personal. What a student wants to say can be said in the inquiry group. What he wants to read, write, and do within the school's curricular and resource limits are bridled only by the student's effort.

For the staff flexible scheduling can provide the framework toward the development of a nongraded school program. A nongraded program allows the student to move through the curriculum at his own rate and, at the same time, makes depth and breadth study possible on an individual basis. Before a school program can be nongraded, the basic content offered by the school must be identified and put in a sequence. Variations from this straight-line sequence are encouraged and even instituted by the teacher as he works with each student individually.

While a nongraded program may be a school staff's goal, it is unrealistic to view it as a twin of flexible scheduling. Perhaps the nongraded school should be organized subsequently to the flexible schedule. Once teachers teach the way the flexible schedule implies, the institution of the nongraded program may follow with relative facility. Of course, it will add a new load to the staff's professional study, cooperation, and decision-making. The IndiFlexS model is structured to accommodate the use of a nongraded high school organization.

## Firming Up the Master Schedule

The tentative master schedule can be firmed up after all the class assignments have been made. Changes, if any, made during the process of matching students to sections can be adjusted on the schedule of each teacher concerned. Once this is done, the schedule can be typed, reproduced, and bound for distribution to the staff.

As the year goes on changes may be made in the master schedule, as well as in student schedules. This is both to be expected and applauded. Changes which are well grounded in professional consideration indicate that professional decisions are being made. Perhaps it is best to think of all scheduling as tentative. Since the rate at which students learn varies and because added familiarity with students by teachers will offer a new insight into individual learning needs, the school's organization for learning should be expected to reflect these developments as the year progresses. Change is a rule of life. The school's organization for learning should respect it.

# PART IV

# SCHEDULES, STUDENTS, AND THE FUTURE

## CHAPTER 12

# One Step: Flexible Scheduling

THE ENGAGING CHALLENGE for today's educator is to develop an organization for instruction which nurtures a quest for learning and helps each youngster to learn more about himself and the world of ideas. Whatever is done in ordering a student's day in school must be the result of serious thinking about the most appropriate way to involve the student in the process of understanding ideas and in developing intellectual skills. The school schedule should be the product of total faculty study and the manifestation of how the teachers believe individual students can be served best. The focus of all the efforts of the school program and personnel must be on each individual student, and the schedule is the vehicle for getting this job done.

Flexible scheduling puts a new premium on the teacher's individual worth. No longer is the teacher an interchangeable part in a standard machine where one qualified teacher can be substituted for another with relative ease. The flexible schedule is built on the competencies and on the recommendations of the teachers within each particular school. Every teacher shapes the program, adds strength to strength, and counts mightily in the determination of what the students, one by one, will be encouraged to investigate and learn.

*Methods Count*

The methods of teaching used in any school are critical. Poor methods usually lead to students inadequately developed in the learning pro-

149

cess. Good methods of teaching help insure depth and breadth learning by each young adult. The flexible schedule is the first step in improving the manner in which teachers teach and the way students learn. Once a school has established a flexible schedule, an intensive, extensive, and continuing in-service education program must be carried out in the school to focus on teaching methods. The full force of the flexible schedule will lose its impact if new teaching methods do not accompany the change to the new schedule.

When one reflects on the really great teachers one has had, one remembers them not only for what they knew, but also for the way they charged thinking and generated production. The methods of teaching used in the flexible schedule put stress on involvement, on reading, on writing, on creating, on reconstructing, and on reflecting.

Successful learning is an active process. Therefore, the school program should be geared to a uninterrupted sequence of student activity. While students will be quasi-active part of the time, the proportion of time spent on this activity will be greatly reduced from the prominent role it plays in today's school. Knowing about a subject is important, but any accumulation of knowledge should be assembled only as a guide to action. Knowing facts alone will not result in either a satisfying or productive life. Both satisfaction and productivity result when those knowledgeable in science become scientists, when those who understand economics become businessmen, or when those who know about literature become authors. The thrill of personal discovery should not be dulled by demands of senseless repetition which are too often a part of a meaningless rigor in outdated instruction. Instead, students should be helped to gain personal satisfaction in the use to which they put the facts they learn and the ideas they discover.

On the ledger of a good school, methodology is balanced by vital content and electrified by intelligent teachers. If the methods of instruction a teacher uses are faulty, the knowledge the teacher transmits is missed by the student. A brick wall of resistance separates interest and understanding. Ignorance persists.

Understanding subject matter is one thing and knowing how to teach it is quite another. Pointed questioning, careful listening, and provocative suggesting are skills the really good teacher must add to his storehouse of knowledge. It is hard to imagine any teacher who has transmitted all he knows to his students in such a way that his knowledge is their knowledge. Conversely, it is not difficult to picture great ideas held by poor teachers who have had little success in sharing their understandings. Procedures used in teaching are influential in the yield of the learning process.

Teaching is much more than talking. The flexible schedule provides some time for essential teacher-centered content presentations. At the same time, it gives needed attention to provisions for student-centered discussions, individual investigation, and practice in using ideas and reconstructing concepts. The schedule is constructed so teachers have the time to meet in small groups and individually with students. What traditional schedule allows these helpful tutorial conferences to take place as a part of the regular school day?

### Curriculum's Companion

Increasingly interest mounts in curriculum development on all levels of the educational system and in most subject-matter fields. New developments are to be expected in extending the humanities in public secondary schools. Mathematics, science, and foreign languages have felt the touch of a helping hand from scholars, professional organizations, foundations, and government-financed agencies. Other content areas are being considered for scrutiny and revision.

A remarkable transformation has been made in some areas of the secondary school. Many good schools have incorporated new understanding of the content of biology, physics, chemistry, and mathematics; accompanying changes have been made in the way these subjects are taught and learned. The process of involvement characterized by these subjects comes from the same theory that undergirds flexible scheduling. The new approaches used in modern foreign language courses are related to increased use of the content and, more important, to the methods of instruction employed. Again, this enlightened approach to instruction in the languages is parallel to the flexible schedule.

If the humanities are to get more attention in the schools, it cannot be by deleting English, social studies, mathematics, science, or the practical arts. Yet the urgency for more attention to the humanities is real to produce a truly educated society. The flexible schedule makes the addition of new content mechanically possible. The flexible schedule is a supporting companion to the emerging curriculum.

As technology finds its way into the school, students will need the time to profit from the advantage of self-operated language laboratories, electronic tape instruction, and programmed learning materials. The flexible schedule can provide the opportunity to use these effectively on an individual basis.

Developing a nongraded school program is an easy and reasonable extension of the flexible schedule. In such a school program students move from subject to subject without the restrictions of artificial grade levels. Progress is determined by individual accomplishment, not by the calendar's promotion dates.

The pressure to give added emphasis, to increase content considerations of other subjects, and to improve the quality of present instructional practice means that changes need to be made in the school's organization for learning. One answer may be to extend the school year to accommodate the additions needed for the youngster in the modern world. Another and perhaps more practical and immediate response to the bulging pressure for content addition is to eliminate useless repetition from some courses and require students to spend less time with others. These utilizations of time can be realized with a flexible schedule.

### Why IndiFlexS?

All that has been done in the development of IndiFlexS has been done to focus attention on the education of each youngster in the modern secondary school. An eye was kept on limited purses so that the proposals made would be within the financial capability of any school district. Also, the proposals made kept the previous training and experience of the contemporary teacher in mind. IndiFlexS is not intended as an idealistic document impossible to use in real situations. With thoughtful study, candid discussion, and cooperative effort involving everyone in the school's network, some form of IndiFlexS can be implemented in any school.

The retooling phase from the traditional to the flexible schedule will require time, patience, and cooperation. The rewards, it is prophesied, will outstrip the sacrifices for the staff. Teaching will take on a new importance when increased individual consideration is given to every student. For the teachers the total personal satisfactions possible from this are inestimable.

IndiFlexS is beamed at the slow student as well as the able and ambitious learner. It is adaptable to those who have a deprived cultural background as well as to those from homes of affluence. In itself, IndiFlexS is both nothing and everything. Even when well-organized, it is nothing if the instructional procedures do not change to focus on the individual student. It can mean everything a developed, inquiring mind can offer if it is properly used.

IndiFlexS is not a final model. Hopefully, it provides a take-off point for others to evaluate, refine, and improve. The fact that it is a working model for any secondary school gives it some general flaws that its application in particular situations may correct. As new curricula finds its way in the school, the schedule can be modified to complement it.

### But How?

Much of the current literature in education, perhaps this book included, is in the form of exhortations. Plea upon plea is made for this or that change. Few constructive proposals have been made that encompass the total school program. Little has been known or written about the change process within the school itself. More attention needs to be given to the problem of program development on the building level.

Some helpful steps can be reported that have been taken by others who have made changes in their organization for learning. The first requirement for any thoughtful staff consideration is to establish a planned program for change. Goals and means to reach them need to be spelled out in detail. Faculty meetings are good vehicles for general discussions. However, they need to be followed up with small group discussions, perhaps on a department by department basis. During these sessions teachers can exchange ideas and crystallize their feelings about the proposals advanced.

It is wise and even necessary to supply teachers with a rich fund of literature on the topic. Usually there is more interest in articles and books which recount what other schools have done than in abstract or theoretical expositions. Special bulletins which give excerpts from the literature are helpful for busy teachers.

Each school should make it a point to encourage teachers to attend national professional meetings. Much can be learned outside the home school district. And most national professional meetings give some attention to flexible scheduling. Reports made to the entire staff by the person who attended a convention are aids in developing a staff's understanding.

Another productive way to spread information is to arrange for the teachers to visit a school doing some form of flexible scheduling. Teachers are influenced by what they see in other schools and hear from other teachers. The time spent in traveling to the school to be visited generally is spent on discussions of the home school. The ride home often is consumed with discussions of the school visited. It is an untested contention that teachers who visit another school usually go away with the idea that they could go home and do the thing they saw and do it better.

At the top of the list of activities to inaugurate a flexible schedule would be a summer workshop. During this time teachers could explore the concept, discuss its application in detail, plan a program, and try out some of the new teaching techniques which are a part of teaching in a flexible schedule. Boards of education would do well to consider the use of some of their funds for program improvement through summer workshops.

Consultants can play a valuable role in setting up a flexible schedule. The consultant may bring fresh ideas and new procedures to bear on solving local problems. There is a mystique that surrounds the consultant. His whims and limitations are veiled while his thoughts are weighed carefully. The consultant can meet with teachers individually to answer nagging personal questions. He can carry on group discussions and bring candor and objectivity to a situation in which he is neither personally nor previously involved. Most important, the qualified consultant can report the experiences of others as he outlines the optional alternatives in actually scheduling the school.

## For Whom?

It is difficult to predict how many schools will use IndiFlexS or some other form of flexible scheduling over the next decade. Those knowledgeable about the concept and convinced of its potential value to teachers and worth to students would hope that the number would be large. The history of change in education makes this unlikely. Changes effected in the schools usually go at the pace of the tortoise, seldom at the speed of the hare. Based on past precedent, the worth of the concept of flexible scheduling will not be a factor in influencing the spread of its use. Instead, attention given it by national professional associations, colleges of education, state departments of public instruction, foundations, and, most important, some educational improvement agency of the federal government will play the major role in determining its use throughout the country. This is in the order of changes in education. Conferences, workshops, consultants, and literature are all needed to get from theory to practice in flexible scheduling. In the end, the use of the concept will be determined by the force of a combination of efforts from a variety of these sources. No single agency by itself can influence the local schools enough to bring about universal uses of flexible scheduling.

The interest in flexible scheduling was kindled first by the National Association of Secondary School Principals. Various other professional organizations, too numerous to mention, have included the topic in their state and national meetings and made reference to it in their journals. A number of state departments of public instruction have given approval to pilot projects. Many, though unfortunately still too few, colleges of education have given passing attention to the ideas involved in flexible scheduling. The Fund for the Advancement of Education and the Educational Facilities Laboratories have included the topic in some of their widely read literature. Still the effort has not been concerted or detailed in explaining the concept and, equally important, giving educators the guides to the techniques of constructing a flexible schedule. If this ever should happen, the use of flexible scheduling may sweep the land. There will then be changes in the courses of colleges of education, in the instructional materials required and used in the schools, and perhaps in both the satisfaction and status of the teachers.

Significantly, the survey of schools for the development of Indi-FlexS indicated that none of those using some form of flexible scheduling wants or expects to abandon it. Most indicated they were planning to expand its use. Scores of others will be added to the list of those using a flexible schedule of one sort or another. This is a certainty. But to predict the extent of its universal acceptance is folly at this point in time.

## *One for Another*

There are those who will maintain that the use of IndiFlexS is the substitution of a new rigidity for an old one, imposed by the traditional schedule. They may say that IndiFlexS is not flexible, but that it presents only complicated variations in the use of time and in the organization of learning groups. This may be a partially valid objection if the IndiFlexS model is not altered and changed frequently. As the teachers see the need for adjustments in the school schedule, they should be made.

When a school uses IndiFlexS for the first semester, the schedule may not undergo wholesale changes. It will take teachers time to become accustomed to working with assembly groups and inquiry groups and to nurture independent study. But once the faculty develops a sense of familiarity with the new methods of teaching in the varying class-size schedule, periodic schedule changes will be called for as a consequence of the teachers' intimate knowledge of students' eduational needs.

IndiFlexS can be changed each week, each month, or each semester. Of course, if the scheduling is done by the hand method, the task will be more time-consuming than if the speed of data processing is available.

Even if one IndiFlexS model is used without adjustment for a semester or a year, it gives great promise for instructional effectiveness. Inquiry-group instruction, properly developed, can have advantage over the degree of student involvement possible in a traditionally organized class. Well-prepared assembly-group instruction, benefited by the added time for teacher preparation, should be more effective than single group lectures repeated four or five times a day. Perhaps most important of all is the time IndiFlexS provides for the individual student to do independent study. Here the student works at his own rate and on subjects in his own sphere of interest.

It is expected that adjustments will be made in the schedule from time to time. Even without them, though, the variations built into IndiFlexS make this form of organization potentially beneficial.

IndiFlexS implies a new relationship between teacher and learner. There is a close bond developed between a teacher and student in the inquiry group which can become a rich experience for the student. Teachers are able to focus instruction at the particular level of the student interest through counsel given in independent study.

Perhaps there are teachers who consistently give the fifth presentation of content as well as the first. There might be teachers who would not profit from additional preparation time. Maybe there are students who get a full measure of individual help from teachers outside their class work. It could be that classes are small enough in some schools for students to be highly involved and to participate often in discussions where ideas are tested and beliefs are verified. Even a casual observer in most schools would have to admit these possibilities usually do not exist. The traditional schedule is an inhibiting factor. IndiFlexS, on the other hand, offers advantages for teachers to utilize their time and talent in a new and more helpful manner for each individual student.

Those who do not want any structure for teaching will not be satisfied with IndiFlexS. Total flexibility, without any scheduling, assumes there are few advantages in group instruction. The IndiFlexS model assumes benefits come from weaving a tightly knit group of students together to work cooperatively on learning problems. Also, the assumption is made in IndiFlexS that some predetermined amount of time in every course can be used for content presentation and summary, for testing, for viewing films, and for learning through other quasi-active experiences.

IndiFlexS is a model that provides variations and affords flexibility but requires an organization to facilitate learning. The organization is determined by the teachers' professional judgment of what is the best way for each youngster to learn. School-wide regulations imposed by the traditional schedule give way to individual requirements for learning in IndiFlexS. The structure of IndiFlexS recognizes that learning involves listening (the assembly group), questioning and discussing (the inquiry groups), and individual activity (independent study). Together these three elements provide an instructional mix. One without the others will not yield the desired formula for quality education.

*Appendices*
*Selected Bibliography*
*Notes*
*Index*

# 1. THE SCHOOLS IN THE SURVEY

Thirty-three schools were surveyed as a part of the preparation of IndiFlexS. Each school was asked to fill out a structured questionnaire and to provide descriptive materials of the school's program. While the respondents were overwhelmingly in favor of the flexible scheduling concept, they were candid and generous in reporting problems and concerns. These were seriously considered in the formulation of IndiFlexS.

The schools and the administrators from whom additional information can be received are listed below. This is in no way a complete list of schools using some form of flexible scheduling but it does include examples of a wide range of the application of the concept in varying degrees.

Arvada West High School, Jefferson County, Colorado
    Principal: Arthur Ohanian
Barrington High School, Barrington, Illinois
    Principal: J. Walter Gillis
Brigham Young University School, Provo, Utah
    Principal: Edward Reed
Brookhurst Junior High School, Anaheim, California
    Principal: Gardner Swenson
Campus High School, Wichita, Kansas
    Principal: Neil Young
El Dorado High School, El Dorado, Arkansas
    Principal: Harold E. Smith
Evanston Township High School, Evanston, Illinois
    Superintendent: Lloyd J. Michael

Fontana High School, Fontana, California
Principal: W. Lloyd Johns
Fremont High School, Sunnyvale, California
Administrative Assistant to the Superintendent: Collins T. Haan
Glenbrook South High School, Glenview, Illinois
Principal: Syd Salt
Holland High School, Holland, Michigan
Principal: Fred S. Bertsch, Jr.
James Madison High School, San Diego, California
Principal: William Jack Stone
James Monroe High School, Bronx, New York
Principal: Oscar Dombrow
Julius West Junior High School, Rockville, Maryland
Principal: L. D. DuBois
Lakeview High School, Decatur, Illinois
Principal: William Fromm
Lincoln High School, Stockton, California
Principal: Ellis T. Mertins
Marshall High School, Portland, Oregon
Principal: Gaynor Petrequin
Mary Potter High School, Oxford, North Carolina
Principal: J. V. Morris
Meadowbrook Junior High School, Newton, Massachusetts
Principal: Betina King
Newton High School, Newton, Massachusetts
Principal: Richard Mechem
New York City Schools, New York, New York
Acting Assistant Superintendent: Jacob B. Zak
Nova High School, Ft. Lauderdale, Florida
Principal: Arthur Wolfe
Palo Alto High School, Palo Alto, California
Principal: Ray P. Ruppel
Pelham High School, Pelham, New York
Principal: William Russell
Penn High School, Mishawaka, Indiana
Principal: Robert Jones
Poway High School, Poway, California
Principal: James Olivero
Ridgewood High School, Norridge, Illinois
Superintendent: Eugene Howard
Senn High School, Chicago, Illinois
Principal: Benedict Amar
Shawnee Junior High School, Lima, Ohio
Principal: Harold Kindy
South Hills High School, Covina Valley, California
Principal: Joe Deal
University School, The University of Chicago, Chicago, Illinois
Principal: Willard Congreve

Virgin Valley High School, Mesquite, Nevada
  Principal: Blaine W. Allan
William C. Overfelt High School, San Jose, California
  Principal: Louis J. Harbor

## 2. JUNIOR-SENIOR HIGH SCHOOL IndiFlexS ORGANIZATION DATA

The IndiFlexS model presented here is for a combination junior-senior high school or for a junior high school of six hundred students in grades seven, eight, and nine and a senior high school with the same number of pupils in grades ten, eleven, and twelve. Increases would be made proportionately in inquiry-group classes, particularly as the enrollment goes up. It is assumed that the distribution of girls and boys is equal on each grade level.

The school day in this model, as recommended in IndiFlexS, is divided into fifteen modules of time for both junior and senior high school students. The courses and the arrangement of learning groups are given as a model. Each subject is organized into a year's course unless otherwise noted. This does not mean, however, that all students will stay in the course for a full year. Some will finish earlier than others. There will be high mobility, particularly in senior high school, between inquiry groups.

ENROLLMENT

| Year in School | | Boys | Girls | Total |
|---|---|---|---|---|
| 7th Year | | 100 | 100 | 200 |
| 8th Year | | 100 | 100 | 200 |
| 9th Year | | 100 | 100 | 200 |
| | Total | 300 | 300 | 600 |
| 10th Year | | 100 | 100 | 200 |
| 11th Year | | 100 | 100 | 200 |
| 12th Year | | 100 | 100 | 200 |
| | Total | 300 | 300 | 600 |

## JUNIOR HIGH SCHOOL ORGANIZATION

### Grades 7, 8 and 9

| Courses | Required | Elective | Meetings Per Week — Inquiry Group | Meetings Per Week — Assembly Group | Meetings Per Week — Medium Group | Modules Per Meeting — Inquiry Group | Modules Per Meeting — Assembly Group | Modules Per Meeting — Medium Group |
|---|---|---|---|---|---|---|---|---|
| **Art Department** | | | | | | | | |
| Art, Drawing | 7 | | 1 | 1 | | 4 | 1 | |
| Art, Crafts | | 7 | | | 2 | | | 3 |
| Art, Ceramics | 8 | | 2 | 1 | | | | |
| Art, Crafts | | 8 | | | 2 | | | 3 |
| Art, History | | 9 | 2 | 2 | | 3 | 1 | |
| Art, Projects | | 9 | 1 | | | 5 | | |
| **Business Dept.** | | | | | | | | |
| Basic Bus. Prin. | 9 | | 1 | 2 | | 2 | 1 | |
| Gen. Bus. Pract. | | 9 | 2 | 1 | | 2 | 1 | |
| Typing | 9 | | | 3 | 1 | | 2 | 2 |
| **English Dept.** | | | | | | | | |
| Eng. I, Slow Lrn. | 7 | | 3 | 2 | | 2 | 1 | |
| Eng. I, Reg. | 7 | | 3 | 2 | | 2 | 1 | |
| Eng. I, Acc. | 7 | | 3 | 2 | | 2 | 1 | |
| Eng. II, Slow | 8 | | 3 | 2 | | 2 | 1 | |
| Eng. II, Reg. | 8 | | 3 | 2 | | 2 | 1 | |
| Eng. II, Acc. | 8 | | 3 | 2 | | 2 | 1 | |
| Eng. III, Slow | 9 | | 3 | 2 | | 2 | 1 | |
| Eng. III, Reg. | 9 | | 3 | 2 | | 2 | 1 | |
| Eng. III, Acc. | 9 | | 3 | 2 | | 2 | 1 | |
| **For. Lang. Dept.** | | | | | | | | |
| French I | | 7, 8, or 9 | 2 | 2 | | 2 | 1 | |
| French II | | 8 or 9 | 2 | 2 | | 2 | 1 | |
| French III | | 9 | 3 | 2 | | 2 | 1 | |
| Spanish I | | 7, 8, or 9 | 2 | 2 | | 2 | 1 | |
| Spanish II | | 8 or 9 | 2 | 2 | | 2 | 1 | |
| Spanish III | | 9 | 3 | 2 | | 2 | 1 | |
| Russian I | | 7, 8, or 9 | 2 | 2 | | 2 | 1 | |
| Russian II | | 7 or 8 | 2 | 2 | | 2 | 1 | |
| Russian III | | 9 | 3 | 2 | | 2 | 1 | |
| **Guidance Dept.** | | | | | | | | |
| Guidance, 7th | 7 | | 2 | 1 | | 1 | 1 | |
| Guidance, 8th | 8 | | | 1 | | | 1 | |
| Guidance, 9th | 9 | | 1 | 1 | | 2 | 1 | |
| **Homemaking, Dept.** | | | | | | | | |
| Homemaking, I | 7 | | 2 | 1 | | 3 | 1 | |
| Homemaking, II | | 8 | 2 | 1 | | 3 | 1 | |
| Homemaking, III | | 9 | 3 | 2 | | 3 | 1 | |
| **Indus. Arts Dept.** | | | | | | | | |
| Indus. Arts I | | 7 | 2 | 1 | | 3 | 1 | |
| Indus. Arts II | 8 | | 2 | 1 | | 3 | 1 | |
| Indus. Arts III | | 9 | 4 | 2 | | 3 | 1 | |

| CONTINUED: | | | Meetings Per Week | | | Modules Per Meeting | | |
|---|---|---|---|---|---|---|---|---|
| Courses | Required | Elective | Inquiry Group | Assem-bly Group | Medium Group | Assem-bly Group | Inquiry Group | Medium Group |
| *Mathematics Dept.* | | | | | | | | |
| Math. I, Slow Lrn. | 7 | | 3 | 3 | | 2 | 1 | |
| Math. I, Reg. | 7 | | 3 | 2 | | 2 | 1 | |
| Math. I, Acc. | 7 | | 2 | 2 | | 2 | 1 | |
| Math. II, Slow | 8 | | 3 | 2 | | 2 | | |
| Math. II, Reg. | 8 | | 3 | 2 | | 2 | | |
| Alg. II, Acc. | 8 | | 2 | 3 | | 2 | 1 | |
| Gen. Math. III Slow | 9 | | 3 | 2 | | 3 | 1 | |
| Alg. III, Reg. | 9 | | 2 | 3 | | 2 | 1 | |
| Alg. Geom. III, Acc. | 9 | | 2 | 3 | | 2 | 1 | |
| *Music Department* | | | | | | | | |
| Gen. Music I | 7 | | | 3 | | | 1 | |
| A Band | | 7-8 | | 2 | | | 3 | |
| B Band | | 7-9 | | 2 | | | 3 | |
| Chorus, 7th | | 7 | 2 | 2 | | 1 | 2 | |
| Vocal Spec. Grps. 7th | | 7 | 2 | 2 | | 1 | 2 | |
| Orches. 7 and 8 | | 7-8 | 3 | | | | 2 | |
| Gen. Music II | 8 | | | 3 | | | 1 | |
| A Band | | 7-8 | | 2 | | | 3 | |
| B Band | | 7-8 | | 2 | | | 3 | |
| Boys Chorus, 8th | | 7-8 | | | 3 | | 1 | |
| Girls Chorus, 8th | | 7-8 | | | 3 | | 1 | |
| Vocal Spec. Grps. 8th | | 8 | 3 | | | | 1 | |
| Orches. 7 and 8 | | 7-8 | 3 | | | | 2 | |
| Concert Band | | 8-9 | 2 | 2 | | 2 | 2 | |
| Boys Chorus, 9th | | 9 | | | 3 | | 1 | |
| Girls Chorus, 9th | | 9 | | | 3 | | 1 | |
| Vocal Spec. Grps. 9th | | 9 | 3 | | | | 1 | |
| *Phys. Ed. Dept.* | | | | | | | | |
| Girls I | 7 | | 2 | 2 | 1 | 2 | 3 | 1 |
| Boys I | 7 | | 2 | 2 | 1 | 2 | 3 | 1 |
| Girls II | 8 | | 2 | 2 | 1 | 2 | 3 | 1 |
| Boys II | 8 | | 2 | 3 | 1 | 2 | 3 | 1 |
| Girls III | 9 | | 2 | 2 | 1 | 2 | 3 | 1 |
| Boys III | 9 | | 2 | 3 | 1 | 2 | 3 | 1 |
| *Science Dept.* | | | | | | | | |
| Science I, Slow Learner | 7 | | 2 | 2 | | 3 | 1 | |
| Science I, Reg. | 7 | | 2 | 2 | | 3 | 1 | |
| Science I, Acc. | 7 | | 3 | 3 | | 2 | 1 | |
| Science II, Slow | 8 | | 2 | 3 | | 2 | 1 | |
| Science II, Reg. | 8 | | 2 | 3 | | 2 | 1 | |
| Biology II, Acc. | 8 | | 2 | 2 | | 3 | 1 | |
| Gen. Sci. Slow | 9 | | 2 | | | 2 | 4 | 1 |
| Biology, Reg. | 9 | | 2 | 2 | 1 | 3 | 4 | 1 |
| Phy. Sci. Acc. | 9 | | 1 | 4 | 3 | 1 | 1 | 4 |

| CONTINUED: Courses | Required | Elective | Meetings Per Week | | | Modules Per Meeting | | |
|---|---|---|---|---|---|---|---|---|
| | | | Inquiry Group | Assembly Group | Medium Group | Inquiry Group | Assembly Group | Medium Group |
| *Social Studies Department* | | | | | | | | |
| Soc. Stud. I, Reg. | 7 | | 3 | 2 | | 3 | 1 | |
| Soc. Stud. II Cult. Dep. | 7 | | 2 | 3 | | 2 | 1 | |
| Soc. Stud. II Acc. | 7 | | 3 | 2 | | 2 | 1 | |
| Soc. Stud. II Slow | 7 | | 2 | 2 | | 2 | 1 | |
| Soc. Stud. II Reg. | 8 | | 4 | 2 | | 2 | 1 | |
| Soc. Stud. II Cult. Dep. | 8 | | 2 | 3 | | 2 | 1 | |
| Soc. Stud. II Acc. | 8 | | 2 | 3 | | 2 | 1 | |
| Soc. Stud. II Slow | 8 | | 2 | 3 | | 2 | 1 | |
| Soc. Stud. III Reg. | 9 | | 3 | 3 | | 2 | 1 | |
| Soc. Stud. III Cult. Dep. | 9 | | 2 | 4 | | 2 | 1 | |
| Soc. Stud. III Acc. | 9 | | 2 | 4 | | 2 | 1 | |
| Soc. Stud. III Slow | 9 | | 2 | 4 | | 2 | 1 | |
| Soc. Stud. III Reg. | 9 | | 2 | 4 | | 2 | 1 | |

### SENIOR HIGH SCHOOL ORGANIZATION

## Grades 10, 11 and 12

| Courses | Required | Elective | Meetings Per Week | | | Modules Per Meeting | | |
|---|---|---|---|---|---|---|---|---|
| | | | Inquiry Group | Assembly Group | Medium Group | Inquiry Group | Assembly Group | Medium Group |
| *Art Dept.* | | | | | | | | |
| Modern Art | 11 | | | 1 | | | 1 | |
| Painting | | 10, 11 & 12 | 2 | | | 3 | | |
| 3-D Design | | 11 or 12 | | | 2 | | | 2 |
| Ceramics | | 10, 11 & 12 | | | 3 | | | 2 |
| Adv. Art | | 11 or 12 | 2 | | | 4 | | |
| Art Seminar | | 12 | 2 | | | 2 | | |
| *Bus. Ed. Dept.* | | | | | | | | |
| Intro. to Bus. | | 10, 11 or 12 | 2 | 3 | | 2 | 1 | |
| Typing ( 1 sem. ) | 10 if not before | | 1 | 2 | | 1 | 2 | |
| Adv. Typ. ( 1 sem. ) | | 11 or 12 | | | 3 | | | 2 |

| CONTINUED: | | | Meetings Per Week | | | Modules Per Meeting | | |
|---|---|---|---|---|---|---|---|---|
| Courses | Required | Elective | | Assem- | | | Assem- | |
| | | | Inquiry Group | bly Group | Medium Group | Inquiry Group | bly Group | Medium Group |
| Shorthand | | 11 or 12 | 3 | 2 | | 2 | 1 | |
| Salesmanship | | | | | | | | |
| (1 sem.) | | 10-11 | 3 | 2 | | 2 | 1 | |
| Bus. Law (1 sem.) | | 11-12 | 2 | 3 | | 2 | 1 | |
| Economic Theory | 12 | | 1 | 2 | | 2 | 1 | |
| Transcription | | 12 | 4 | | | 2 | | |
| Office Occup. | | 12 | scheduled for one half-day on the job | | | | | |
| Distributive | | | | | | | | |
| Educ. | 11-12 | 11-12 | scheduled for one half-day on the job | | | | | |
| *English Dept.* | | | | | | | | |
| Speech | | 11 or 12 | 3 | 1 | | 3 | 1 | |
| Drama | | 12 | 2 | 2 | | 4 | 1 | |
| Journalism | | 10, 11 & 12 | 2 | 1 | | 2 | 1 | |
| Eng. IV, Slow | 10 | | 3 | 2 | | 2 | 1 | |
| Eng. IV, Reg. | 10 | | 3 | 2 | | 2 | 1 | |
| Eng. IV, Acc. | 10 | | 2 | 3 | | 2 | 1 | |
| Eng. V, Slow | 11 | | 3 | 1 | | 3 | 1 | |
| Eng. V, Reg. | 11 | | 3 | 2 | | 2 | 1 | |
| Eng. V, Acc. | 11 | | 2 | 2 | | 2 | 1 | |
| Eng. VI, Slow | 12 | | 3 | 2 | | 3 | 1 | |
| Eng. VI, Reg. | 12 | | 3 | 2 | | 2 | 1 | |
| Eng. VI, Acc. | 12 | | 2 | 3 | | 2 | 1 | |
| Eng. Seminar | | 11-12 | 3 | | | 2 | | |
| *For. Lang. Dept.* | | | | | | | | |
| French I | | 10 | 3 | 2 | | 2 | 1 | |
| French II | | 10, 11 or 12 | 2 | 3 | | 2 | 1 | |
| French III | | 10, 11 or 12 | 3 | 2 | | 2 | 1 | |
| French IV | | 11 or 12 | 3 | 3 | | 2 | 1 | |
| French V | | 11 or 12 | 3 | 3 | | 2 | 1 | |
| Spanish I | | 10 | 3 | 3 | | 2 | 1 | |
| Spanish II | | 10, 11 or 12 | 2 | 3 | | 2 | 1 | |
| Spanish III | | 10, 11 or 12 | 3 | 3 | | 2 | 1 | |
| Spanish IV | | 11 or 12 | 2 | 3 | | 2 | 1 | |
| Spanish V | | 11 or 12 | 2 | 3 | | 2 | 1 | |
| Russian I | | 10 | 3 | 2 | | 2 | 1 | |
| Russian II | | 10, 11 or 12 | 3 | 2 | | 2 | 1 | |
| Russian III | | 10, 11 or 12 | 2 | 3 | | 2 | 1 | |
| Russian IV | | 10, 11 or 12 | 2 | 3 | | 2 | 1 | |
| Russian V | | 11 or 12 | 2 | 3 | | 2 | 1 | |
| Language Sem. | | 12 | 3 | | | 3 | | |
| *Guidance Dept.* | | | | | | | | |
| Social Guid. | 10 | | | 2 | | | 1 | |
| Voc. Guid. | 11 | | | 1 | | | 1 | |
| Educ. Guid. | 12 | | | 1 | | | 1 | |
| *Homemaking Dept.* | | | | | | | | |
| Clothing (1 sem.) | | 10 or 11 | 1 | 2 | | 6 | 1 | |
| Foods (1 sem.) | | 10 or 11 | 2 | 3 | | 4 | 1 | |

| CONTINUED:<br>Courses | Required | Elective | Meetings Per Week | | | Modules Per Meeting | | |
|---|---|---|---|---|---|---|---|---|
| | | | Inquiry Group | Assembly Group | Medium Group | Inquiry Group | Assembly Group | Medium Group |
| Family Living | | 12 | 2 | 2 | | 3 | 1 | |
| Modern Home | | 11 or 12 | 2 | 1 | | 4 | 1 | |
| Seminar | | 11 & 12 | 2 | | | 1 | | |
| Family Issues | 12 | | 1 | 2 | | 2 | 1 | |
| *Indus. Arts Dept.* | | | | | | | | |
| Drafting | | 10 or 11 | | | 2 | | | 4 |
| Mechanics | | 11 or 12 | | 2 | 1 | | 1 | 5 |
| Electricity | | 11 or 12 | 1 | | 2 | 2 | | 4 |
| Cabinet Making | | 10 or 12 | | | 1 | | | 7 |
| Diversified Occup. | | 11 & 12 | scheduled for one half-day on the job | | | | | |
| Modern Industry | 11 | | 1 | 2 | | 2 | 1 | |
| Arranged Proj. | | 11 or 12 | 2 | | | | 1 | |
| *Math. Dept.* | | | | | | | | |
| Consumer Math. | | 10 or 11 | 3 | 2 | | 2 | 1 | |
| Bus. Math. | | 11 or 12 | 2 | 4 | | 2 | 1 | |
| Pl. Geom. | | 10 | 3 | 2 | | 2 | 1 | |
| Adv. Algebra | | 11 | 2 | 3 | | 2 | 1 | |
| Trigonometry | | 12 | 2 | 3 | | 3 | 1 | |
| Math. Seminar | | 11-12 | 2 | | | 2 | | |
| *Music Dept.* | | | | | | | | |
| Music Apprec. | 10 | | 1 | 1 | | 1 | 1 | |
| Band, Concert | | 10, 11 & 12 | 1 | | 3 | 2 | | 2 |
| Band, Marching | | 10, 11 & 12 | 1 | | 3 | 2 | | 2 |
| Orchestra | | 10, 11 & 12 | 1 | | 2 | 2 | | 3 |
| Instr. Ensem. | | 10, 11 & 12 | 1 | 2 | | 3 | 2 | |
| Choir | | 11 & 12 | 1 | 3 | | 1 | 1 | |
| Chorus, Concert | | 10, 11 & 12 | 1 | 2 | | 2 | 1 | |
| Boys Choir | | 10, 11 & 12 | 1 | 3 | | 1 | 1 | |
| Girls Choir | | 10, 11 & 12 | 1 | 3 | | 1 | 1 | |
| Music Theory | | 11 or 12 | 2 | | 2 | 2 | | 2 |
| Music Projects | | 11 & 12 | 2 | | | 1 | | |
| *Phys. Ed. Dept.* | | | | | | | | |
| Boys, IV | 10 | | 1 | 2 | 2 | 2 | 1 | 2 |
| Girls, IV | 10 | | 1 | 2 | 2 | 2 | 1 | 2 |
| Boys, V | 11 | | 1 | 2 | 2 | 2 | 1 | 2 |
| Girls, V | 11 | | 1 | 2 | 2 | 2 | 1 | 2 |
| Boys, VI | 12 | | 1 | 2 | 2 | 2 | 1 | 2 |
| Girls, VI | 12 | | | 2 | 2 | 2 | 1 | 2 |
| Health, I | 10 | | 1 | 1 | | 2 | 1 | |
| Health, I | 10 | | 1 | 1 | | 2 | 1 | |
| Health, II | 11 | | 1 | 2 | | 2 | 1 | |
| Projects | | 11 & 12 | | | | | | |
| *Science Dept.* | | | | | | | | |
| Biology | | 10 | 2 | 3 | 1 | 2 | 1 | 5 |
| Earth-Air Sci. | | 10 or 11 | 2 | 3 | 2 | 3 | 2 | |
| Physics | | 11 | 2 | 3 | | 4 | 1 | |
| Chemistry | | 11 or 12 | 1 | 3 | | 6 | 1 | |

| CONTINUED:  Courses | Required | Elective | Meetings Per Week | | | Modules Per Meeting | | |
|---|---|---|---|---|---|---|---|---|
| | | | Inquiry Group | Assem- bly Group | Medium Group | Inquiry Group | Assem- bly Group | Medium Group |
| Electronics | | 12 | 1 | 2 | | 4 | 1 | |
| Adv. Biology | | 10 or 11 | 1 | 3 | | 3 | 1 | |
| Science Proj. | | 12 | 2 | | | 1 | | |
| Soc. Stud. Dept. Sociology (1 sem.) | | 10 or 11 | 3 | 2 | | 2 | 1 | |
| Anthropology (1 sem.) | | 10 or 11 | 2 | 3 | | 3 | 1 | |
| World History | | 10 or 11 | 2 | 4 | | 2 | 1 | |
| 20th Cent. Trends | 12 | | 2 | 2 | | 2 | 1 | |
| U.S. History | 11 | | 2 | 2 | | 2 | 1 | |
| Special Projects | | 10, 11 or 12 | 2 | | | 1 | | |
| Seminar | | 11 & 12 | 1 | | | 3 | | |

For a comparison of the staffing requirements and enrollment distribution in a junior-senior high school, see David W. Beggs' *Decatur-Lakeview High School: A Practical Application of the Trump Plan* (Englewood Cliffs, N.J.: Prentice-Hall, 1964), pp. 231-244.

## 3. STAFF REQUIREMENTS FOR THE INDIFLEXS MODEL

The wisest utilization of professional talent is one of the purposes of IndiFlexS. While no formula assembled for a model school program will have application in a particular school, it might be helpful to have an example given of the staff requirements when IndiFlexS is used. Below are the staff requirements for the junior-senior high school mentioned throughout this book. These requirements for professional staffing are for a school of 1,200 students with the pattern of courses as given in Appendix Two.

A full teaching load includes 60 modules of instruction or assignment for work with the teaching teams, for supervision of special activities, for work with individual students, and for regular class teaching.

*Art Department:*
    108 modules of assigned instruction required per week    2 teachers
    (1 teacher assigned to the junior high and 1 teacher assigned to the senior high with membership on one team.)
*Business Education Department:*
    201 modules of assigned instruction required per week    4 teachers

(There will be some additional time available in this department for working with independent study projects.)

*English Department:*

589 modules of assigned instruction required per week  11 teachers
(There will likely be six teaching teams, one for each grade level.)

*Foreign Language Department:*

149 modules of assigned instruction required per week  3 teachers
(Since there is only one teacher for each of the three languages offered, team organization is not possible. Each teacher would teach in both the junior and senior high schools.)

*Guidance Department:*

83 modules of assigned group meetings for the junior high school and 4 modules of assigned assembly-group meetings per week in the senior high are only a part of the counselors' load. Because of the vital role counselors play in this program the number of counselors needed may exceed the number usually in a school of this size                                          5 counselors
(Two counselors likely would be assigned to the junior high school and three to the senior high school.)

*Homemaking Department:*

104 modules of assigned instruction required per week  2 teachers

*Industrial Arts Department:*

161 modules of assigned instruction required per week  3 teachers

*Instructional Materials Center :*

No regular teaching assignments                        1 librarian

*Mathematics Department:*

427 modules of assigned instruction required per week  8 teachers
(There will probably be two junior high school teams and two senior high school teams.)

*Music Department:*

112 modules of assigned instruction required per week  2 teachers
(One teacher will probably handle the vocal classes, the other the instrumental classes and both the general music and appreciation classes.)

*Physical Education Department:*

219 modules of assigned instruction required per week  5 teachers
(An athletic director is included in this department's

staff requirements. The athletic director would likely be the department head and teach only 16 modules a week. Driver education classes for the behind-the-wheel phase would be taught during the summer and the driver education theory would be taught during the school year.)

*Science Department:*

| | |
|---|---|
| 396 modules of assigned instruction required per week | 7 teachers |

(Two teams would be organized in the junior high school division and the other three teachers would teach in the senior high school.)

*Social Studies Department:*

| | |
|---|---|
| 438 modules of assigned instruction required per week | 9 teachers |

(Four teams of two teachers each would be needed. Two teams each in the junior and senior high school with another teacher handling the advanced courses.)

*School Administration:*

| | |
|---|---|
| Principal | 1 |
| Assistant Principals | 2 |
| Director of Student Activities | 1 |

*Noncertified Teachers' Aides:*

| | |
|---|---|
| General Typists | 2 |
| Audiovisual Specialist | 1 |
| Records Clerk | 1 |
| Teachers' Correction Clerks | 2 |
| Principal's Secretary | 1 |
| Assistant Principals' Secretary | 1 |
| General Office Recorder | 1 |
| Guidance Department Secretary | 1 |
| Instructional Materials Center Clerks | 3 |
| Total Noncertified Staff | 13 |

## 4. MODEL STUDENT AND FACULTY SCHEDULES

Six schedules—three for teachers and three for students—are given as examples. Each is intended to reflect one aspect of the range of variation possible with the use of IndiFlexS.

Notice that the amount of time devoted to independent study increases from the seventh to twelfth grades. The need for frequent inquiry and assembly groups diminishes as the student matures and develops study skills. During independent study time students are free to consult teachers as needed.

The variations in content and learning activities are made within each inquiry group with the assembly-group time used for broad content exposition, testing, resource speakers, and some audiovisual presentations. The schedule cannot show all the content variations or methods of teaching used from group to group. It does show the amount of time and group size used for each subject.

While custom schedules are made for each student, the principles which are guidelines for each student's schedules are the same, as discussed in Part One.

The teachers' schedules indicate both the assigned classes and the optional activities. Teachers who work with the inquiry groups are free to attend the assembly classes or to do something else during these periods.

Each teacher's and each student's schedule probably will be different from every other teacher's and student's schedule in the school. Thus, the typical schedule is difficult to sketch because of the infinite range of variations which exist between schedules.

A SEVENTH GRADE GIRL'S SCHEDULE
WITH INDIFLEXS

| Time | Monday | Tuesday | Wednesday | Thursday | Friday |
|------|--------|---------|-----------|----------|--------|
| 8:30 | Art, 7th (Assembly Group) | Science, 7th (Assembly Group) | English, 7th (Inquiry Group) | Soc. Stud. 7th (Inquiry Group) | Science, 7th Assembly Group) |
| 9:00 | Guidance, 7th (Inquiry Group) | Soc. Stud. 7th (Inquiry Group) | | | Soc. Stud. 7th (Inquiry Group) |
| 9:30 | | | Homemaking, 7th (Assembly Group) | | Independent Study |
| 10:00 | Math. 7th (Assembly Group) | | Independent Study | Math. 7th (Assembly Group) | |
| 10:30 | Independent Study | Independent Study | | English, 7th (Inquiry Group) | English, 7th (Assembly Group) |
| 11:00 | Music, 7th (Assembly Group) | English, 7th (Assembly Group) | Music, 7th (Assembly Group) | | Music, 7th (Assembly Group) |
| 11:30 | L | U | N | C | H |
| 12:00 | English, 7th (Inquiry Group) | Math. 7th (Inquiry Group) | Spanish, 7th (Inquiry Group) | Spanish, 7th (Inquiry Group) | Spanish, 7th (Inquiry Group) |
| 12:30 | | | | | |
| 1:00 | Spanish, 7th (Assembly Group) | Guidance, 7th (Assembly Group) | Math. 7th (Inquiry Group) | | Math. 7th (Inquiry Group) |
| 1:30 | Science, 7th (Inquiry Group) | Art, 7th (Inquiry Group) | | Spanish, 7th (Assembly Group) | |
| 2:00 | | | Independent Study | Homemaking, 7th (Inquiry Group) | Science, 7th (Inquiry Group) |
| 2:30 | | | | | |
| 3:00 | Phys.Educ.7th (Assembly Group) | | Phys.Educ.7th (Assembly Group) | | |
| 3:30 | Independent Study | | Art Project· | | Art Project |

This student does well in all of the regular courses and is gifted in art.

### A TWELFTH GRADE GIRL'S SCHEDULE
### WITH INDIFLEXS

| Time | Monday | Tuesday | Wednesday | Thursday | Friday |
|---|---|---|---|---|---|
| 8:30 | Office Occup. (Inquiry Group) | On the Job | On the Job | On the Job | Office Occup. (Inquiry Group) |
| 9:00 | | | | | |
| 9:30 | | | | | |
| 10:00 | English, VI (Inquiry Group) | | | | Family Issues 12th (Inquiry Group) |
| 10:30 | | | | | |
| 11:00 | Independent Study | | | | Independent Study |
| 11:30 | Econ. Theory 12th (Assem. Group) | English, VI (Assembly Group) | Guidance, 12th (Assembly Group) | Econ. Theory 12th (Assem. Group) | English, VI (Assembly Group) |
| 12:00 | L | U | N | C | H |
| 12:30 | On the Job | Family Issues 12th (Assem. Group) | Independent Study | Family Issues 12th (Assem. Group) | On the Job |
| 1:00 | | Independent Study | | Independent Study | |
| 1:30 | | | Econ. Theory 12th (Inquiry Group) | | |
| 2:00 | | | | | |
| 2:30 | | | English, VI (Inquiry Group) | Independent Study | |
| 3:00 | | | | | |
| 3:30 | | | Independent Study | English, VI (Inquiry Group) | |

This school girl is in the work-study Office Occupations Program. She spends her mornings in school on Monday and Friday and works in a retail store office in the afternoon and evenings. She also works on Tuesday, Wednesday, and Thursday mornings and attends classes in the afternoon on these days.

A NINTH GRADE BOY'S SCHEDULE
WITH INDIFLEXS

| Time | Monday | Tuesday | Wednesday | Thursday | Friday |
|---|---|---|---|---|---|
| 8:30 | English, 9th (Inquiry Group) | Independent Study | English, 9th (Inquiry Group) | Soc. Stud. 9th (Assembly Group) | English, 9th (Inquiry Group) |
| 9:00 | | | | Independent Study | |
| 9:30 | Independent Study | Math. III (Inquiry Group) | Guidance, 9th (Assembly Group) | Math. III (Inquiry Group) | Soc. Stud. 9th (Inquiry Group) |
| 10:00 | | | Soc. Stud. 9th (Assembly Group) | | |
| 10:30 | Math. III (Assembly Group) | English, 9th (Assembly Group) | Math. III (Assembly Group) | English, 9th (Assembly Group) | Math. III (Assembly Group) |
| 11:00 | L | U | N | C | H |
| 11:30 | Ind. Arts III (Assembly Group) | Typing (Assembly Group) | Ind. Arts III (Assembly Group) | Typing (Assembly Group) | Guidance, 9th (Inquiry Group) |
| 12:00 | Boys Chorus 9th (Medium Group) | | Boys Chorus 9th (Medium Group) | | |
| 12:30 | Independent Study | Phys. Ed. 9th (Assembly Group) | Independent Study | Phys. Ed. 9th (Assembly Group) | Math. III (Inquiry Group) |
| 1:00 | Soc. Stud. 9th (Assembly Group) | Soc. Stud. 9th (Inquiry Group) | | Independent Study | |
| 1:30 | Phys. Ed. 9th (Inquiry Group) | | | | |
| 2:00 | | Ind. Arts III (Inquiry Group) | Phys. Ed. 9th (Medium Group) | Ind. Arts III (Inquiry Group) | Phys. Ed. 9th (Inquiry Group) |
| 2:30 | Typing (Medium Group) | | | | |
| 3:00 | | | | | Soc. Stud. Special Help |
| 3:30 | English Special Help | | English Special Help | | Boys Chorus 9th (Inquiry Group) |

This student is a slow learner in English and Social Studies but learns easily and does well in other subjects.

## AN ELEVENTH GRADE ENGLISH TEACHER'S SCHEDULE
### WITH INDIFLEXS

| Time | Monday | Tuesday | Wednesday | Thursday | Friday |
|---|---|---|---|---|---|
| 8:30 | Planning | Planning | Planning | Planning | Planning |
| 9:00 | | | | | |
| 9:30 | | | | | |
| 10:00 | Journalism (Inquiry Group A) | Journalism (Inquiry Group D) | Journalism (Assembly Group) | Journalism (Inquiry Group A) | Journalism (Inquiry Group D) |
| 10:30 | | | Instructional Materials Center Consultation | | |
| 11:00 | Journalism (Inquiry Group B) | Journalism (Inquiry Group E) | | Journalism (Inquiry Group B) | Journalism (Inquiry Group E) |
| 11:30 | | | | | |
| 12:00 | L | Department Duties | | C | Department Duties |
| 12:30 | School Newspaper Staff Meeting | U | N | Principal's Cabinet | H |
| 1:00 | | Journalism (Inquiry Group F) | School Yearbook Staff Meeting | | Journalism (Inquiry Group F) |
| 1:30 | Journalism (Inquiry Group C) | | | Journalism (Inquiry Group C) | |
| 2:00 | | Journalism (Inquiry Group F) | Planning | | Journalism (Inquiry Group F) |
| 2:30 | Department Duties | | Department Duties | Department Duties | |
| 3:00 | | Department Duties | | | Department Duties |
| 3:30 | | | | | |

This teacher works with the journalism classes and is chairman of the English Department. Since there is only one journalism teacher, he is not a member of a team.

## AN EIGHTH GRADE MATHEMATICS TEACHER'S SCHEDULE
## WITH INDIFLEXS

| Time | Monday | Tuesday | Wednesday | Thursday | Friday |
|---|---|---|---|---|---|
| 8:30 | Math. II (Inquiry Group A) | Planning | Math. II (Inquiry Group A) | Planning | Math. II (Inquiry Group A) |
| 9:00 | | | | | |
| 9:30 | Math. II (Inquiry Group B) | Algebra, 8th (Inquiry Group A) | Math. II (Inquiry Group B) | Algebra, 8th (Inquiry Group A) | Math. II (Inquiry Group B) |
| 10:00 | | | | | |
| 10:30 | Math. II (Assembly Group) | Algebra, 8th (Inquiry Group B) | Algebra, 8th (Assembly Group) | Algebra, 8th (Inquiry Group B) | Algebra, 8th (Assembly Group) |
| 11:00 | Math. II (Inquiry Group C) | | Math. II (Inquiry Group C) | | Math. II (Inquiry Group C) |
| 11:30 | | Algebra, 8th (Inquiry Group C) | | Algebra, 8th (Inquiry Group C) | |
| 12:00 | L | | N | | H |
| 12:30 | Team Meeting | U | Team Meeting | C | Team Meeting |
| 1:00 | Math. II (Inquiry Group D) | Special Help Class Math. II | Math. II (Inquiry Group D) | Special Help Class Math. II | Math. II (Inquiry Group D) |
| 1:30 | | Algebra, 8th (Inquiry Group D) | | Algebra, 8th (Inquiry Group D) | |
| 2:00 | Planning | | Planning | | Planning |
| 2:30 | | Math. II (Assembly Group) | | Math. II (Assembly Group) | |
| 3:00 | Math. II (Inquiry Group E) | Algebra, 8th (Inquiry Group E) | Math. II (Inquiry Group E) | Algebra, 8th (Inquiry Group E) | Math. II (Inquiry Group E) |
| 3:30 | | | | | |

This teacher works with inquiry groups.

A TENTH GRADE WORLD HISTORY TEACHER'S SCHEDULE
WITH INDIFLEXS

| Time | Monday | Tuesday | Wednesday | Thursday | Friday |
|---|---|---|---|---|---|
| 8:30 | World History (Assembly Group) | World History (Assembly Group) | World History (Assembly Group) | World History (Assembly Group) | Instructional Materials Center Consultation |
| 9:00 | Planning | Planning | Planning | Planning | |
| 9:30 | | | | | World History (Inquiry Gr. Seminar A) |
| 10:00 | World History (Inquiry Group A) | Instructional Materials Center Consultation | World History (Inquiry Group A) | Instructional Materials Center Consultation | |
| 10:30 | | | | | |
| 11:00 | World History (Inquiry Group B) | | World History (Inquiry Group B) | | |
| 11:30 | | | | | Planning |
| 12:00 | Team Meeting | Special Projects | Special Projects | Team Meeting | |
| 12:30 | L | U | N | C | H |
| 1:00 | World History (Inquiry Group C) | Planning | World History (Inquiry Group C) | Planning | World History (Inquiry Gr. Seminar B) |
| 1:30 | | | | | |
| 2:00 | World History (Inquiry Group D) | World History (Inquiry Group E) | World History (Inquiry Group D) | World History (Inquiry Group E) | |
| 2:30 | | | | | |
| 3:00 | Planning | World History (Inquiry Group F) | Planning | World History (Inquiry Group F) | Planning |
| 3:30 | | | | | |

This teacher is responsible for the assembly-group instruction and serves as the teaching team chairman.

# SELECTED BIBLIOGRAPHY

The purpose of this bibliography is to provide a variety of data sources on the wide range of considerations related to flexible scheduling although not specifically on the topic.

Anderson, Vernon E., and William T. Gruhn. *Principles and Practices of Secondary Education.* New York: Ronald Press, 1962.
This book is a valuable reference for the in-service educator, as well as for the student of professional secondary education. Part III, on school organization, and Part IV, on improvement practices, are especially noteworthy.

A.S.C.D. Commission on the Education of Adolescents. *The High School We Need.* Washington, D.C.: Association for Supervision and Curriculum Development, National Education Association, 1959.
This booklet may stand for several decades as a classic in setting forth sound recommendations for improved schools.

Austin, David, and Noble Gividen. *The High School Principal and Staff Develop the Master Schedule.* New York: Columbia University Press, 1960.
This discussion of scheduling is not specifically related to flexible scheduling, but it does highlight some of the considerations for school scheduling generally.

Beggs, David W. *Decatur-Lakeview High School: A Practical Application of the Trump Plan.* Englewood Cliffs, N.J.: Prentice-Hall, 1964.
The experiences of a junior-senior high school which used flexible

179

scheduling, team teaching, and other innovations are reported. The procedures used to bring about the school's new program are discussed.

———, ed. *Team Teaching: Bold New Venture*. Bloomington: Indiana University Press, 1964.

Team teaching as it applies to both secondary and elementary schools is considered in depth in this analysis of the concept. Practical suggestions are made for implementing team teaching.

——— and Edward G. Buffie, eds. *Independent Study: Bold New Venture*. Bloomington: Indiana University Press, 1965.

This volume concentrates on one aspect of flexible scheduling, independent study. It develops several models of school organizations to facilitate its use.

Brown, Frank B. *The Non-Graded High School*. Englewood Cliffs, N.J.: Prentice-Hall, 1963.

A plea for breaking the lockstep of secondary school education with reference to the program at Melbourne High School in Florida is given by its principal.

Bush, Robert N., and Dwight W. Allen. *A New Design for High School Education*. New York: McGraw-Hill, 1964.

This book discusses flexible scheduling rationale, theory, and alternate options. The reasons for developing a flexible schedule are forcefully stated and soundly reasoned.

Corey, Stephen M. *Helping Other People Change*. Columbus: Ohio State University Press, 1963.

This is one of the Kappa Delta Pi lectures. Curriculum workers and supervisors will profit from Dr. Corey's experiences and recommendations.

Cram, David. *Explaining Teaching Machines and Programming*. San Francisco: Fearon Publishers, 1961.

By means of using a learning program, this book does a splendid job of explaining and demonstrating programmed learning techniques.

Erickson, Erik H., ed. *Youth: Challenge and Change*. New York: Basic Books, 1963.

A group of perceptive contributors have written candidly about the problems and pressures on youth in the twentieth century. This book is helpful as a staff establishes its instructional objectives.

Fliegler, Louis A., ed. *Curriculum Planning for the Gifted*. Englewood Cliffs, N.J.: Prentice-Hall, 1961.

While written primarily for elementary school teachers, high school teachers will find this book helpful in early curriculum planning for the gifted.

Gardner, John W. *Excellence.* New York: Harper & Brothers, 1961. Quality education is discussed by Dr. Gardner in clear terms. Part Three is of particular interest in its discussion of individual differences.

Heath, Robert W., ed. *New Curricula.* New York: Harper & Row, 1964. Heath has edited a significant book which reports on the major curricular innovations and projects on the current scene. This should be discussed by every school faculty.

Kephart, Newell C. *The Slow Learner in the Classroom.* Columbus, Ohio: Charles E. Merrill, 1960. A body of curriculum recommendations are made to provide helpful and productive learning activities for slow learners.

Miles, Matthew B., ed. *Innovation in Education.* New York: Columbia University Press, 1964. This volume contains a collection of papers on the process of change in education. While the quality is uneven, the book contains some helpful ideas about changing school programs and teaching practices.

Murphy, Judith, and Robert Sutter. *School Scheduling by Computer: The Story of Gasp.* New York: Educational Facilities Laboratories, Inc., 1964. This is an important publication in the field of scheduling. Scheduling a flexible organization by data processing is clearly and completely described. The book reports the work done by Robert Holz at the Massachusetts Institute of Technology on developing a data processing program for a flexible schedule.

N.E.A. Center for the Study of Instruction. Project on Instruction. *Education in a Changing Society.* Washington, D.C.: National Education Association, 1964. One of three volumes produced by the Project on Instruction, this is pointed in making recommendations to change the schools in a constructive and helpful way. Every school should have this volume and perhaps the other two in the series in its professional library.

Riessman, Frank. *The Culturally Deprived Child.* New York: Harper & Row, 1962. Some of the central issues facing American public school educators concerning culturally deprived students. The author does a scholarly job of penetrating analysis on this vital subject.

Trump, J. Lloyd. *Images of the Future*. Washington, D.C.: National Association of Secondary-School Principals, National Education Association, 1959.

Both in the prose and in the diagrams in this booklet, Dr. Trump presents his recommendations for the beneficial changes that need to be made in secondary education.

———— and Dorsey Baynham. *Guide to Better Schools: Focus on Change*. Chicago: Rand McNally, 1961.

This book presents the full range of staff utilization concepts in clear, easy-to-read language. It is important enough for every teacher to read it from cover to cover.

# NOTES

## CHAPTER 4

1. David W. Beggs, III, *The Decatur-Lakeview High School: A Practical Application of the Trump Plan* (Englewood Cliffs, N.J.: Prentice-Hall, 1964), pp. 27-42.

## CHAPTER 5

1. For a discussion of team teaching operation, see *Team Teaching: Bold New Venture,* ed, by David W. Beggs, III (Bloomington: Indiana University Press, 1964).

## CHAPTER 6

1. Educational Facilities Laboratories, Inc., 477 Madison Avenue, New York, N.Y., will provide information about new facility plans to accommodate a flexible schedule.

2. See *Instructional Materials Center: Bold New Venture* (to be published by Indiana University Press) for a more complete description.

## CHAPTER 7

1. Taken from an address by Donald C. Manlove at the annual meeting of the North Central Association of Colleges and Secondary Schools, Chicago, Ill., April 8, 1964.

2. For a review of the related research, see Robert H. Anderson, "Organizational Character of Education: Staff Utilization and De-

ployment," Chapter V, *Review of Educational Research* 34:455-469, October, 1964.

3. David W. Beggs, *The Decatur-Lakeview High School,* pp. 3-4.

## CHAPTER 8

1. Roughly sixty teachers for each 1,200 junior high school students and sixty teachers for each 1,000 senior high school students, including administrative and other professional personnel.

# Index

185